# BUFFETS AND REWARDS

THE WORKMAN AND HIS TOOLS

# BUFFETS
## and
# REWARDS

*An autobiographical record (1937–1951)*

S. P. B. MAIS

*With 26 Illustrations*

HUTCHINSON
LONDON

Hutchinson & Co. (Publishers) Ltd.
London, New York, Melbourne, Sydney, Cape Town

*First published 1952*

Printed in Great Britain
by The Anchor Press, Ltd.,
Tiptree, Essex

With all my love and deep gratitude to

JILL

LALAGE

IMOGEN

PENELOPE (Blithe Spirit)

and

BROTHER LISTENER

Who encouraged me in widely diverse ways

to

Finish the Last Lap

"I strove with all, for all were worth my strife:
Nature I fought, and, after Nature, Man.
I burnt both hands before the fire of life:
It sinks, and I'm among the 'Also Ran'."

                              W. S. LANDOR (almost)


"Stiff in opinions, always in the wrong:
Was everything by starts, and nothing long."

                              JOHN DRYDEN


"No man was ever written down but by himself."

                              SAMUEL JOHNSON


"I wish you wouldn't decry yourself so.
People might believe you."

                              MY MOTHER


"Speak of me as I am: nothing extenuate,
Nor set down aught in malice."

                              *Othello*


"I always eat my grapes downwards lest I
should die before I reach the best."

                              SAMUEL BUTLER


"An autobiography is the only book in which
Truth does not matter."

                              LESLIE STEPHEN

# CONTENTS

# LIST OF ILLUSTRATIONS

# CHAPTER I

## I Dine with the Sette of Odd Volumes (1951)

### § 1

"And sign it," I shouted into the telephone, "sign it 'Mais', M (pause) A (pause) I (pause) S (pause) S for sugar."

"Will you turn that radio down?" I yelled to Lalage, who was with her friend Jasper in the dining-room. "I'm trying to telephone."

"No one but you would have the telephone in the hall," replied Lalage spiritedly.

"You're awfully easy on the eye," blared the radio crooner from my study.

"That'll be meant for you, Doreen," I shouted to the telephone operator.

"None of your sauce, young man," shouted the operator. "My name's Ireen, anyway."

"Good night, Ireen, Ireen, good night," I sang. "Don't go, sweetheart," I said. "Thank you for that word 'young'. It's lucky it's not television. I'm sixty-five, my hair is white, my weight is 13 stone 12 lb. And I look smashing in a beard. Could you spare the time to read my telegram over?"

"It would serve you right if I didn't," shouted the operator. "Can you hear me?"

"No," I said, "but I'll have you sacked, Gertie, if you don't. I'm the Postmaster-General."

"Norman Birkett," read the operator, "Royal Courts of Justice, Strand. Stop. Yes. Stop. Coming to Odd Volumes if I have to borrow white tie from Dean. Stop. Love and kisses. Stop. Mace. Stop."

"No, no, no," I shouted. "Mais, Maze, like Indian corn, not Mace. M (pause) A (pause) I (pause) S (pause) S for Sugar."

"Two S's?"

"One, Flossie, one."

"That's a funny name. Never heard of it."

"You break my heart, Cissie. I bet your Mum and Dad knew it, if you have a Mum and Dad."

"Anything else?"

"My heart cries for you," I sang.

would rush at him as soon as he opened his mouth and flappers would swoon and surge round for his autograph."

"Why?" said my elder daughter.

"Because, my sweet," I said, "believe it or not, I was a popular and quite well-known broadcaster. I was what the *Daily Express* called an 'ace', almost as well known as Wilfred Pickles is now."

"What's that got to do with S for Sugar?"

"He didn't have to spell his name and hear people call him Mace. As soon as he spoke, wherever he went, people would nudge each other and say 'That's S. P. B.' He resents the eclipse."

"What happened?" asked Lalage.

"War," I said. "And old age. I'm now a 'Ham'. No come-back for me. I'm out."

"Anything less like a ham," said Jill, "I never saw."

"It can't be old age," said Lalage. "They like old age on the air. They're always applauding old women because they're eighty or ninety, as if they'd just made a century in a Test."

"Sixty-five doesn't count. They just forget your existence. You wouldn't believe that I used to have a fan-mail of about a couple of hundred letters a day."

"I wouldn't," said Jill. "You once got one hundred when you said you liked whiskey. They weren't polite."

I disregarded that.

"Now I get only bills and letters beginning 'Unless'."

"It must be fun having a famous father," said Lalage wistfully.

"You needn't rub it in."

"All the same, I wish you were. How did you become famous?"

"Having three initials."

"Seriously."

"Falling in the Three-Mile race against Cambridge, twice."

"You didn't really get a Blue?"

"Two."

Lalage went into a sort of trance.

"Fancy your being a Blue."

"Well, if one's own daughter doesn't know a thing like that, how do you expect anyone else to remember?"

"And how did you become a famous broadcaster?"

"They mistook me for Christopher Stone."

"Were you a good broadcaster?"

"Excellent."

"Why aren't you on the air now?"

"I told a young lady that she oughtn't to go down a coalmine."

"What's there wrong about that?"

"It's the way your father says things, not the things he says."

"Not always," I said. "It was the things I said that got me sacked from Sherborne and shot out of the R.A.F. It was the thing I wouldn't say that got me sacked from the Press."

"You've still got your books. You can say what you like in books."

"Can you? I said that the service in an hotel we once stayed in was a bit slow. That cost me £800. I said that a seaside village ought to have its drains seen to. The book had to be withdrawn from circulation."

"Oughtn't you to be a bit more careful?"

"If your father was careful he wouldn't be your father," said Jill.

"I'm so hungry that I could eat the tin," said Lalage.

"Probably less harmful to the system than what's inside it," I said. "Let's go."

§ 2

Leaving Lalage and Jasper to wash up Jill and I went off to St. Peter's Hall to see Aldous Huxley's play *The World of Light*. In spite of being desperately tired I kept awake and was delighted.

Before I went out to Switzerland I used to have to sit up till two or even three o'clock in the morning writing my theatre notices. I was now well again. I went to bed as soon as I got home and wrote my notice as soon as I got up next morning.

After finishing my notice I started looking for dress studs, putting them into a dress shirt, looking for dress buttons to put into my dress waistcoat, and brushing the tail coat that I wear only at Odd Volume dinners. I then went down to the kitchen to make my first pot of tea for the morning. That done I went back to my desk and wrote letters telling the Editors of the *Queen*, *Country Life* and *Men Only* that I should be calling at their respective offices within forty-eight hours full of bright ideas. I then tried to think up some ideas that I could sell to them. As I am ill for six months in the year I importune them rarely enough for them to find both my presence acceptable and my suggestions palatable. Gone, thank God, are the days when, like the young Samuel Johnson, I had to wait at the

B

outward doors of editors, like an outpatient in a casualty ward, or was so often repulsed from the office door by an insolent typist with "The Editor's out" or "The Editor can't see you."

I may be no longer famous, but even in Broadcasting House directors of programmes seldom repulse me. They offer me nothing, but they remain disarmingly friendly.

I shouldn't describe myself as a popular man or even likable. I'm nervous and cowardly, yet I have an odd habit of suddenly speaking my mind out about people in high places quite loudly. I have certainly no tact. My life is spent among women. I see very few men. I belong to only one London club, the Odd Volume. I'm absurdly superstitious, but not so superstitious as my Cornish mother, whose day was completely spoilt if she saw a single magpie, and her night ruined if she saw the new moon through glass.

"It'll be all right," I say to myself, "it'll be all right if I get to the lamp-post before the next car catches me up." I usually arrange for a margin of safety.

I bow nine times to the new moon, turn my silver and wish fervently. I pray only on my knees. I am afraid that God won't listen if I pray standing up. When I'm ill the psalms depress me so much that I can't bring myself to go to church. I enjoy church-going when I'm on top of the world. "Fight the good fight" rouses me as the blind ballad-singer roused Sir Philip Sidney. The first chapter of the Epistle of St. James makes my blood surge with delight. Some of the collects fill me with happiness. But when I'm ill I am a monk in reverse. When I am ill I turn my face to the wall and contemplate, not without apprehension, oblivion, annihilation.

I repeat over and over with Charles Lamb:

Sun, and sky, and breeze, and solitary walks, and summer holidays, and the greenness of fields, and the delicious juices of meats and fishes, and society, and the cheerful glass, and candle-light, and fireside conversations, and innocent vanities, and jests, and irony itself—do these things go out with life? Can a ghost laugh, or shake his gaunt sides when you are pleasant with him?

That touches the very root of the matter. I may well be dead when you read this. Shall I be looking over your shoulder and laughing say: "Young man, or more probably, young woman, make the most of it while you have it. Life in any form is good."? You may be afflicted with a stammer like Charles Lamb, damned like Cassio in a fair wife, or like Hazlitt in a foul one, depressed by melancholia like Johnson, by religious mania like Cowper, or a madness that was anything but religious like John Clare. However badly you may have been treated you will agree that life is pleasant and death unpleasant. "When I have fears that I may cease to be." I am constantly haunted by that fear. My contemporaries fall by my side like leaves from a tree after a frost or gale in autumn. They fall, they fade, they are all too soon forgotten, but I remain like the last couple in an Elimination Dance.

I don't want to vanish from your sight until I have said what I came on earth to say, that not only the wind on the heath is pleasant, but that all life is pleasant. I have even known tramps who have unconsciously acted on Johnson's advice and accepted life on the conditions that are offered to them.

I have never really accepted life. My parents were poor and honest. I didn't notice the poverty except when it made my mother lose her temper with my father for sending a packet by letter-post when it would have been cheaper by parcel-post. I cried at that. It seemed to sever their relationship. I am uncertain about honesty. If it is a policy it isn't honesty. There is nearly always a clause in a policy which lets the insurance company out.

If there is an eternity I would rather spend it in the company of some of the rogues whom I have known and loved than among the intolerably tedious honest folk who may well find an eternal satisfaction in twanging a harp in the haunts of a heaven where there is no night.

I am, unlike Walter Savage Landor, not at all ready to depart just because the fire of life sinks. I am most tenacious of what remains, a week, a month, a year, ten years, partly because I enjoy life so much, partly because there is so much more that I want to see and taste, partly because I can't bear the thought of being separated from Jill, Lalage and Imogen, with whom I quarrel violently but grasp to my heart of hearts with hooks of steel.

I know so little, I remember so little. There is so much I want to know, so much I want to remember.

But for you who have all your life still to live, listen to Robert Louis Stevenson, who knew what he was talking about because he was always on the threshold of Death's door:

As courage and intelligence are the two qualities best worth a good man's cultivation, so it is the first part of intelligence to recognize our precarious state in life, and the first part of courage to be not at all abashed before the fact. A frank and somewhat headlong carriage, not looking too anxiously before, not dallying in maudlin regret over the past, stamps the man who is well-armed for this world.

I have never been well-armed. I am no Achilles, vulnerable only in the heel. I can don neither the armour of light nor the breastplate of righteousness. I have always been a too easy target for the powers of darkness, but for some inscrutable reason I am still alive, alive and kicking, kicking against the pricks of convention.

Life has been fun, and however it ends, unless I lose my reason and am no longer able to say what I mean, life has been, as it was with Hazlitt, in spite of all, happy, so happy that I don't want to leave it.

If Heaven has anything better to offer it must be a fine place.

I am not worried about the prospect of the disappearance of sex life in a Hereafter where there is neither marriage nor giving in marriage (what's the difference?), because the ecstasy of sexual consummation is exactly on a parallel with the ecstasy of winning a race or scoring a try. I no longer want to win a race or score a try. And yet I have some physical faculties left. When I have put off this mortality, this corruption of flesh, I hope to attain to a world in which the spirit it untrammelled, and what little I have seen of my spirit (precious little) I quite like.

It's God I'm concerned about, not myself. I don't want too much discipline. I don't want Raphael and Michael to turn out to be infinitely omniscient like a Brigade of Guards sergeant-major. I want leisure to fold my spiritual legs and have my talk out, no longer seeing things through a glass darkly but face to face with a reality that is and certainly ought to be ineffably lovely.

> Into the earth that gave the rose
> Shall I with shuddering fall?

No, not if it is roses, roses all the way.

I comfort myself with Quintilian. I believe because belief is so manifestly impossible. God certainly moves in a most mysterious way His wonders to perform.

When I started this digression I was in my study writing letters to the Editors of the *Queen, Country Life* and *Men Only*, telling them to clear decks for action, hang out the bunting and put down the red carpet. "S. P. B." was on his way.

I had a good deal else to do. There was the typescript of my book on Oxford that I wrote two years ago for a publisher who refused it. For a year it had been lying hidden among a pile of manuscripts on my desk. There was my book on the Channel Islands, written when I was very ill, and refused. I would submit that to somebody. I flourish on refusal when I'm well. It's only when I'm down that I don't much relish being hit and hit again.

There was my novel. On reading it through I was horrified and completely emasculated it.

My publisher's readers were equally horrified and I had been asked to revise it. In my low state I couldn't bear the sight of it and was on the verge of tearing it up when I thought better of it. I now unearthed it and again intended to submit it once more to the original publisher.

I then packed up my ski-ing tunic, trousers and boots to take back to Moss Bros.

While I was in the process of packing (I can't even pack a parcel when I am ill) I thought I heard the latch of my iron gates raised. I peered out into the darkness listening for the crunch of footsteps on the gravel outside my window. I fingered the sharp Highland dagger that I keep on my desk.

Then it occurred to me that if anybody was lurking in the garden with felonious or murderous intent he would be unlikely to attack so strangely dressed a creature as I am. Always in the early morning I wear a Madeira wine-server's skull cap (*capacuca*) on my head, a long blue and white check Christ Church scarf round my neck, a heavy black ski-ing sweater, twill riding breeches, Norwegian sealskin slippers, and a lurid silk dressing-gown of yellow and black.

I am not, I think, odd in any other particular, but I display certain idiosyncrasies in dress. I wear three waistcoats, the outer one a mustard-yellow hunting waistcoat with brass buttons.

I then cleared out the bottom of the grate, threw the ashes into the dust-bin (I like making a good row doing that before dawn), brought in two buckets of coal and then cleaned and polished my shoes ready for the journey.

I had a pile of books to review for the *Oxford Mail* but I felt disinclined to read other men's compositions. I decided to write to Priscilla and Vivien, my two elder daughters, of whom I see nothing and to whom I never write when I'm ill and seldom when I'm well.

Don't run away with the idea that I don't like them. I love them dearly. They have had a hard life. Priscilla, born in 1916, is lovely. She contracted a disease of the leg when she was training to be a dancer in the Russian ballet in Paris.

She married just before the war a Frenchman of whom I know little beyond the fact that he was a Count and drank port in the morning.

On 12th May, 1940, she was in Amiens. So were the Germans. Apparently they treated her reasonably in her first concentration camp. Indeed, she prevailed upon the sentimental German camp doctor to release her on the ground that she was about to have a baby. She was not, of course, about to have a baby. She was indiscreet about this. When they caught her they put her into another concentration camp in the Vosges, where life was much less pleasant.

When I next saw her she had divorced her husband.

She remarried, an Englishman this time who grows strawberries and tomatoes on the Sussex coast. He, too, had already been married and had two small children.

My second daughter, Vivien, who was born in 1920, is equally beautiful in a different way. She spent her war among her own people, so she is still able to laugh easily. But she, too, has had her trials.

At seventeen she married a quiet, capable, music-loving naval officer. He was among those reported missing when H.M.S. *Prince of Wales* was sunk by the Japanese in Singapore Harbour.

Several months later he reappeared and was immediately posted to a destroyer, which shortly afterwards was sunk. He was again reported missing. Again he reappeared, only to be posted to a submarine, which in due course was also sunk and he was once more reported missing.

He must be a hard man to drown.

He again reappeared, and the Admiralty, tired of the monotonous regularity of his reappearances, posted him to Bath, an ironical touch which shows that the Lords of the Admiralty have their humorous side.

For some reason into which I have not enquired (the wise father doesn't even try to know his own child), after producing a perfectly healthy boy, this couple, who are more devoted to each other than any other couple I know, decided to adopt an orphan Czech. It was a Christian act.

I have had considerable luck with my four daughters. I like them all. I am proud of them all. I can't tell you more about the two elder ones, because I don't know any more about them. About my Lalage (twenty) and Imogen (fifteen) you will hear more, but not now.

I am trying to take you to the Savoy to attend with me a dinner of the Sette of Odd Volumes. It is taking longer than I thought. I seem to have adopted a *Tristram Shandy* style. We may never get to the Savoy. It is quite unintentional, I assure you. After all, if you are bored you can always shut the book and go off and have a game of Canasta.

At seven o'clock, or a little before, the world began to stir in its sleep and prepare for the day's work. There was quite a lot of bird-song. The workmen's buses passed. There were lights in the upper windows of the kindergarten school on the other side of the paddock on which I look out across the road. The milkman came, the papers came, I let Simon out. Simon is Jill's Cairn. I let Simon in. Jill came downstairs in her dressing-gown to cook the breakfast which she always eats in her bedroom. I turned the wireless on, took the heavily laden tray upstairs, called Lalage, who is always reluctant to leave her bed, and took my porridge and coffee back to the study where Jill, occupying my big desk, was now typing out my review of the play of the night before.

Then came the postman. I still haven't quite given up the hope that some admirer of my broadcasts of long ago will leave me a substantial fortune, so that I can pay off my overdraft and the many shops who seem unaccountably unwilling to press me for the payment of bills that have been outstanding for years.

Lalage came downstairs to collect my "copy" to take to the Editor on her way to her office. My copy has to be in the Editor's hands by 9 a.m. She is not due in her office until nine-thirty. It is good of her to forgo a half hour of sleep on my behalf, but when she says:

"Can you lend me your pump or light?" I reply with some heat: "Where's yours?"

I watch her go out to the garage, mount her bicycle and ride away. She doesn't wave as Jill does. She is not demonstrative.

I have always been punctilious about time ever since a never-to-be-forgotten occasion when I was an undergraduate. I had made a firm friend of one Douglas McNair, who was neither at the same school nor even at the same college. He was at Charterhouse and New College, I was at Denstone and Christ Church. As a freshman I had made a friend of a red-headed Carthusian called Henry

Lascelles, who was at "The House" with me. It was he who introduced me to Douglas McNair. McNair and I agreed to meet one day at Canterbury Gate, just outside my rooms, at a certain hour on a certain date. I have forgotten for what purpose.

I was, I don't know why, five minutes late. I was surprised at his fury.

"I was just going," he said. "If I had gone I would never have spoken to you again."

Had I been a minute later I should have lost the best friend I ever had.

I have been punctual for every appointment ever since. I have indeed always allowed a margin of time, and I have always been glad.

On this particular morning Lalage left the house at nine o'clock to deliver the typescript of my theatre notice which was due at nine o'clock two and a half miles away.

Our train was due to leave Oxford at 10.15. I had ordered the car for 9.50. Before that I had to wash up the breakfast things. I'm one of the few men in the world who really like washing up. The reason is odd. When I am ill I can't tie up a parcel or buy a stamp. There is only one thing that I can do to my own satisfaction. However ill I am mentally I can still wash up. The result of seeing a dirty plate come clean through my agency always makes me pleased with myself. I have never smashed a glass in sixty-six years.

After washing up I had to take Simon down to Miss Selby, who lives next door but one.

It falls to my lot whenever we leave the house empty for a day or more to put Simon on his lead (no, Jill puts him on the lead), and armed with his dish of food walk down to 287 (we live at 291 Woodstock Road) and deliver him over to the good-natured dog-lover who looks after him in our absence. The car draws up exactly at 9.50. I call up to tell Jill that the car is here.

"I'm just coming," she shouts. "Don't be so impatient."

When Death comes to claim her Jill will say "I'm just coming" and then look into this mirror and that, put on a little more lipstick, pat her hair here and there, and then find that she must go to the lavatory.

We left the house just before ten. We were, of course, in plenty of time. There was time to talk to the ticket collector who has a boy in the R.A.F. who has got a State scholarship to St. Peter's Hall. Ever since we first came back to Oxford in 1941 that collector has told me about that son of his, and how ambitious he has been for him.

Oddly enough I have never met the boy. I hope that he will remember in later life what he owes to his father.

We had coffee in the buffet car going up and I reviewed a novel.

We got to London at 11.30 and trekked out of the exit to Ashton's Hotel, known to all taxi-drivers as "The Load of Hay". The hotels round Paddington have uneven reputations, but Ashton's is ideal. It is quiet, it is close to the station. It is cheap, 17s. 6d. inclusive of bath, bed and breakfast. The service is excellent. Its clientele is mainly West Country. One hears a lot of Welsh spoken. For half an hour I telephoned to various publishers and friends. In three instances the numbers had been changed. In three others the number was engaged, so I was late for my appointment with Staples.

I looked at the pasted-up copy of my book, *Britannia 1651-1951*, and handed in the thousand words or so in which I had epitomized the spirit and outstanding features of London which they required as an appendix to my Middlesex chapter. My idea in this book was, I think, a happy one. It was to reproduce Jansson's 17th-century maps of the English counties and on the page opposite each county map to give an epitome of the county's main points of interest.

Originally I had meant to use Saxton's maps. The only copy of his atlas that I could find was in Cambridge and its price £450. A man in Birmingham offered me an incomplete Speed (it lacked ten of the more popular counties) and I bought it for £135, and then, finding that I couldn't afford it, I sent it back and the bookseller only allowed me £95, a dead loss of £40. Luckily, Wilson, of Victoria Street, had a complete and perfect volume of Jansson's maps, which he let me have for £85, and I let Staples copy these. It took me quite a long time to do these brief summaries of each county, but the effect was worth while because nobody else has had the idea, and I believed that it ought to command a fairly large sale among visitors from overseas. I left behind the typescript of my book on Oxford which they appeared to like, as well as my *Chronicle of English Literature*, which was originally published by Heinemann in 1936.

By one o'clock Jill and I were having luncheon in the Berkeley Buttery. It cost £1 4s. 6d. for the two of us, but the food was excellent, the company pleasant (mainly women) and the service efficient. At three o'clock we were in the handsome offices of the *Queen*, where I induced the Editor to commission an article on Harrogate and another on Amateur Dramatic Societies.

It is only a step from Burleigh Street to Temple House, where

"The fun of the thing. Why not? Some people like taking risks."

He was a loquacious taxi-driver, very, very innocent and very, very young. He went on talking more and more excitedly about the incident. I didn't listen. I was thinking.

"Some people," I had said, "like taking risks." Did I?

Courage, we are told, is the supreme virtue. It is odd that though I pray night and day for energy ("When you're ill," Jill said, "you're as flat as a pancake. When you're well you're just a volcano, and just about as dangerous") I never pray for courage.

I have not often been face to face with death. He is no friend of mine. I am certainly afraid of him.

On 4th August, 1914 (a memorable day), I died under an operation for appendicitis. My heart, the surgeon told me afterwards, stopped beating long enough for him to decide that I was for the scrap-heap. It was only the casual remark of a nurse that brought me back to earth.

The world before 4th August, 1914, and the world after that date are so totally opposed in every way that it meant starting life all over again on a much less pleasant basis. We are much less pleasant people. Tragedy and poverty have not purified our spirits. They have embittered us. We can no longer afford to be charitable. We have descended into Chaos and it doesn't bear thinking about.

Am I courageous? I don't think so. Two incidents that have a curious similarity, though they were separated in time by forty years, are seared into my mind.

One hot summer afternoon in 1907, when I was an undergraduate, I was bicycling down the towpath towards the Long Bridges swimming pool when I saw a young couple who were punting in midstream collide with one of Salter's steamers.

As I am a strong swimmer I always think that other people can swim. I was in a hurry to bathe. I really didn't give them a second thought. After all, the Thames is quite narrow by the college barges, and there were plenty of people about on the river and on the towpath. I went on to my bathe. When I came back I saw their bodies. They were both drowned. I haven't forgiven myself for that yet.

It would not, however, have impressed itself upon my mind so fiercely had it not been for a similar incident in the Summer of 1944.

I was lying on the banks of the Cherwell at the Dragon School bathing-place in my bathing things, basking in the sun, and reading. There were two blondes sitting on the board by the water-side, also in bathing things, giggling fatuously at two G.I.s who, rather surprisingly, were in the water. Americans as a rule find English river-water too cold for their liking. They were cajoling the girls to join them. They were literally pulling their legs and eventually one of the girls fell in. As she was in a bathing costume that seemed to me to be inevitable and natural.

The gigglings increased, and then changed to loud and strident screams. Apparently the girl couldn't swim and the two American soldiers were not by instinct or training life-savers.

I watched the struggle in the water with amusement. I thought the splashing was intentional. Instead of diving in to her rescue I got up and walked away. Agreed that there were dozens of people about who could, and in point of fact did, go to her rescue. That is not the point. The point is this. It flashed across my mind that if I had dived in and in trying to rescue her had lost my life it would have been the waste of a good life. She may have been worthless, and I was still at that time on the air every morning trying to compensate the nation for the bad war news by some gay nonsense about food. The programme, which I invented, was called "The Kitchen Front". It certainly seemed to divert people's attention from the dangerous moment. It elicited thousands of letters of thanks. It also produced a postcard that I have carried in my pocket ever since to restore my spirits when I have been down. It came from a member of the Wallasey Ladies' Golfing Association.

"I have been married," she wrote, "for 20 years, and the first time my husband has ever laughed at breakfast time has been during your morning talks—Thank you!"

There was a laconic postscript from the husband. "Quite true."

Am I a coward? I don't know.

There was an occasion during the war as we were driving Lalage and Imogen back to school at Cheltenham when we came face to face with death and I didn't like it. A heavy Army lorry pulled out from behind a long procession of lorries on a bend of the road as they were going down Andoversford Hill. We were going fast. The lorry was going fast. There seemed to be no possibility of escape. Our driver, a man of my own age, with extraordinary quickness of mind, drove straight over the kerb and up into the hedge. The lorry flashed past. By a miracle we didn't turn over. The car righted itself and in a couple of minutes our hearts returned to normal. That was a bad moment. I pass that spot at the beginning of every term as we take Imogen back to school and always, as we pass, I shudder.

I sweated with fear when my friend John Corlette, who doesn't know the meaning of the word, took us all in his car in Switzerland over icy roads up mountain passes where we skidded from side to side and seemed every other moment to go within a centimetre or two of the edge of precipices. He had no chains and used no brakes.

"When the roads are as bad as this," he said, "you've got to pretend that you're ski-ing."

I sweated with fear with him just as I used to sweat with fear whenever I went out for a drive with my father, who obeyed only his own rules of the road. If he saw a parishioner on the farther pavement he would disregard all traffic, put out no warning hand, but just cross the road. Every lamp-post in his parish looks slightly drunk as the result of being used as a buffer for his car. He never acquired the art of stopping.

Driving with my father was fun if you were feeling well. If you were feeling nervy it was hell. Curiously enough he regarded himself as a perfect driver. His accidents were always due to the other fellow. I was very surprised indeed that he lived to die in his bed.

He, like John Corlette, didn't know the meaning of fear. I am more like my mother, who apprehended danger and disaster everywhere. I am certainly of very little use in a crisis. Only a few weeks ago Jill, who is always experimenting with gas and electricity, detected a leak in a pipe, lit it, and instantly a huge flash of flame came spouting out into the kitchen and threatened to set the house on fire within a few minutes unless we did something drastic.

I completely lost my head.

"Water!" I cried. "Drench it with water!" I ran to the telephone with the idea of ringing up the fire brigade. I couldn't remember what number to dial.

I ran out of the house to my next-door neighbour, who is knowledgeable about houses. By great good fortune he was in and came quickly.

"You've only got to turn the gas off at the main," he said.

"I don't know where the main is," I said miserably.

"You ought to be certified," he said.

I expected to see the house in flames. It wasn't. Jill had stuffed a cork into the pipe and burnt her hands. The walls and tables bore signs of burning.

"Where is the main?" asked our neighbour.

"In the pantry behind the Hoover and a mountain of brown packing paper," said Jill.

It took about ten minutes to find the meter and then I didn't know which lever to pull which way.

I felt very small. In household matters I am amazingly ignorant.

"Any other man I ever met," says Jill frequently, "can at least change an electric bulb, mend a fuse, use a chisel and screwdriver. I never met a man so useless with his hands. You can't even do anything in the garden."

"I can wash up, and I can bring in the coal, and light a fire."

"You can't even sew on a button or mend your own socks. Your father——"

"My father could whitewash a house inside and out, rear hens and ducks, cultivate a garden, drive a car, cook a dinner, take a swarm of bees, remove fungus as well as look after a parish, and preach a sermon. Some people have all the gifts. I have but one."

"And that is?"

"The capacity to keep my temper when my ignorance of all arts and crafts is pointed out to me."

"I can't think how you've got through life knowing so little about so much."

I've never sought popularity, that last infirmity of ignoble minds, but quite a large number of boys whom I have educated showed a genuine and lasting affection for me.

I don't seem to have many firm friends. People don't ask me out much. When the telephone rings it is invariably an invitation to a cocktail party for Lalage, never for me. The truth is that Jill and I have been pretty well inseparable ever since we first met twenty-eight years ago. We always walk together, eat together, and go to the flicks together, as well as sleep together. When I'm away from her she is lost. When she is away from me I am lost. I can't think what we're going to do in the next life if we don't coalesce.

I've devoted so large a proportion of this life trying (in vain) to make both ends meet that I shan't know what to do in a world where things are no longer assessed on an economic basis. It'll be odd enough not to have any more marriage. It will be odder not to have to chase about trying to earn enough to pay for my daily bread.

I often wonder how my very godly father and gawdly (she always said "Gawd") mother are faring.

Anything is better than annihilation. Dear God, please don't annihilate me. I think my spirit is worth encouraging. There's a touch of divinity about it. I'm sorry that it's so dim, but don't on that account snuff it out altogether like a candle.

I'm taking an unconscionable time reaching Fitzroy Street. That is because the taxi-driver's mind still ran so much on the smash-and-grab raid that he overran Number 4, and we drove up and down its entire length several times before locating the office that I was looking for.

On my arrival Redman handed me the advance copies of my book *Madeira Holiday*.

I have written about 145 books (there's nothing meritorious about that), but I still have an ecstatic moment when I first open a new book of mine and wonder what its fate will be.

Nearly all books are soon forgotten, but I go on hoping that one day I shall write one that will not be quickly forgotten.

I was pleased with everything about *Madeira Holiday* except its rather commonplace coloured dust-jacket. In the old days I used to instruct the artist and tell him exactly what I wanted. I am becoming less finicky about this. That is a mistake, because booksellers tell me that attractive dust-jackets have been responsible for more sales than any author would imagine. I know that I am attracted first by the dust-jacket when I loiter by the bookstalls on station platforms.

My day's work was over. I felt very tired. I took a taxi from Tottenham Court Road back to Ashton's Hotel and spent the next hour shaving, changing and rehearsing my speech for the Sette of Odd Volumes dinner.

As the whole object of this lengthy chapter is to introduce you to the Sette of Odd Volumes let me now tell you something about it.

It has no premises. We meet at the Savoy on the fourth Tuesday of alternate months, and we dress in tails and white ties. Once a year we invite ladies.

The Sette was founded by Bernard Quaritch in 1878. It consists of twenty-one members, this being the number of volumes of the Variorum Shakespeare of 1821. Supplemental Odd Volumes may be elected up to the number of twenty-one. We are permitted, even encouraged, to bring guests. These guests are usually well known and of great diversity.

Among the members, to show you how odd and diverse we are, are Alec Waugh, Vyvyan Holland, G. D. Roberts, J. G. Lockhart, Lord Halsbury, Lord Birkenhead, Sir Norman Birkett, Val Gielgud, Denzil Batchelor and Russell Vick. We each have a pseudonym. Mine is Perambulator. Lord Halsbury is Chymicophant, Lord Birkenhead is Faber, and Sir Norman Birkett is Listener.

This was a particularly important occasion as Brother Listener

IMOGEN IN INFANCY

IMOGEN AND JILL

LALAGE PAINTING

PETRE AND LALAGE

PETRE AS SCHOOLMASTER          PETRE AS CRICKETER

IMOGEN AND LALAGE IN DEVON

was down to read a paper on Advocacy. My guests were Basil Blackwell and Nicholas Hannen.

I have already made it clear that my main virtue is punctuality. Like politeness it costs nothing. Indeed, it often saves money and a great deal of trouble. It inspires confidence.

I was in the ante-room of the Banqueting Chamber at 6.45. There was one other occupant. It was Nicholas Hannen, known to his friends as "Beau".

"You're early!" I said.

He smiled graciously.

"You've forgotten how you bit my head off the last time you asked me because I was five minutes late. You've got a vicious tongue. I wasn't going to risk it a second time. What a bully you must have been as a schoolmaster."

"Not at your school," I replied.

"That's one of the few Public Schools from which you weren't sacked. You were never at Radley."

"On the contrary. I was at Radley during the war. It was the only thing left for me to do. The R.A.F. wouldn't have me. The B.B.C. tried me out on food, but not for long. No Ministry wanted me. Not even M.I.5 would look at me."

"It's beastly being over sixty. We might as well be dead. I'm 'r. ting'. There'll be time for that in the grave. I want work."

"Don't we all?"

"Tell me about Radley."

"It's your school."

"I mean, how you got on."

"I didn't. One of my boys spent his maths hour lampooning me in verse. He did it well. He ought to get on."

"You thrashed him within an inch of his life?"

"On the contrary, I congratulated him. It was damned good, so good that I can't forget it. Listen:

> "Fatuously, the glasses dangled
> From the old man's mouth,
> His eyes blinked,
> His scant remaining hairs
> Sweatily glued o'er his ears.
> Is it of death he dreams,
> Or is his nightmare
> Failure to impart
> The last faint flickerings of his art?"

C

"Beau" laughed heartily.

"You made that up," he said.

"I didn't."

"No boy ever said that about you."

"This boy did, and he got it right.

> "Failure to impart
> The last faint flickerings of his art.

It couldn't have been put more neatly or more accurately."

"You didn't like Radley?"

"Does one like following a pack of Beagles to which you once whipped in and find yourself unable even to break into a run? That's what growing old does for one."

"One must accept life on the conditions on which it is offered."

"It's not funny to find that you can't do more than send boys to sleep."

"Apparently you inspired this one to keep awake."

"I prefer love to hate, or, what is much worse, contempt."

Members of the Sette and guests began to trickle in and conversation became general.

I am always hailed with an extraordinary display of friendliness by my fellow Odd Volumes. It makes me feel good. I found myself comparing this geniality and conviviality with the last occasion when I had dined in the company of my fellow men. It was at the Union Club only five weeks before, but what worlds away. It was just before my visit to Switzerland and I had to be bullied by Jill to go in spite of the fact that it was an important occasion.

It was to be the final winding-up meeting of a society to which I felt very proud to belong—"The Survivors", confined to members of Christ Church between 1902 and 1912 who had fought in the 1914–18 war and had come back. Men of our age were ripe for sacrifice at that time, as the war memorial in Christ Church Cathedral demonstrates. I am only alive because of my operation on the very day, as Robb Wilton would say, that war broke out. Only about forty of us came back. Of those forty, twenty more had died in the last thirty years. There were, in fact, only twenty of us left, and nineteen turned up to dinner. The absentee was "Owly" Stable, now a judge.

You may have heard of some of the others. We considered ourselves a good vintage. They included Geoffrey Gilbey; H. A. Gilbert,

who played cricket for Worcestershire and the Gentlemen; Jimmy
Horlick; and C. A. Gladstone (grandson of W. E.). The rest were
landed gentry, Masters of Hounds, and so on.

In spite of the fact that I knew them all intimately, I felt completely out of it. I was feeling like death. I owed the bank over
£2,000 without a chance of ever paying it back. I couldn't write.
I couldn't get a job. I had gone touting round Oxford, asking Basil
Blackwell to give me a job behind his bookshop counter, asking the
Nuffield organization if I couldn't help to publicize cars, the City
Librarian if I couldn't hand out books, the Bodley librarian if I
couldn't paste in slips in the catalogues, my own Dean if there
wasn't something somewhere, anything anywhere. There was
nothing. It is not pleasant to realize that one is not wanted
anywhere.

But the Survivors had £61 left in the kitty to blow on one dinner,
so we decided to meet for the last time and have a final good
feast. It wasn't any earthly use to me. No one noticed that I wasn't
my usual roaring self. I walked from one man to another, nodding,
smiling wistfully, unable to say anything brighter than "I'm fine,
thanks. You look damned young." No terror of prison, bankruptcy
court or the pauper's grave haunted them. Economically, if not
physically, they were sound.

It was an excellent dinner. I accepted things on my plate and
left them untouched. I put my hand over my glass when I was
offered sherry. Champagne flowed. The port was especially good.
I drank nothing. I even refused a cigar. I have a passion for cigars.
We never have speeches. It was, therefore, with great surprise that
I saw our secretary rise and heard him say:

"Gentlemen, I have received a pathetic letter from one of our
number who is threatened with bankruptcy."

That brought me back to life with a start. I was a pretty damned
fool and in my illness forgetful. Had I written to refuse the dinner
on account of my poverty?

"Name," shouted someone.

It was on the tip of my tongue to say "Me."

It was not me. It was a most unexpected person who held a
highly honoured name.

It took less than a minute for us to compose our message of
sympathy and promise of practical help.

I wondered what line the others would take if I rose to my feet
and said:

"Hold hard. I'm another of them. I can't pay my way either. I'm broke too."

I know what they would have done. They would have roared with laughter. They wouldn't have believed me. I have always been extravagant, always lived beyond my means.

The Survivors are an odd lot. They are nearly all Old Etonians or Old Wykehamists. Yet they accepted me as one of themselves. The Etonians took it for granted that I was at Winchester, the Wykehamists that I was at Eton.

Before we broke up, the meeting took an unexpected turn. It may have been the champagne. A member got up and said:

"I realize, gentlemen, that it is out of order to make a speech at a Survivors' Dinner, but I want to say just one thing. I want the Survivors to survive. I see no earthly reason why we should throw our hands in just because our numbers are reduced to twenty. I for one am willing to come up from South Wales until you are all dead. Then I'll dine by myself and drink your healths. We are very closely knit together. We shared an Oxford that has become a myth. We shared a war that was not a myth. We have gone our several ways, but we have too much in common to throw it away. I may as well confess that I look forward to my gossip over this table, talking to men who talk the same language that I talk and share the same interests, more than anything else in the whole year."

It may have been the wine. We decided to carry on *sine die*. I was glad about that. Perhaps at the next meeting I might have come alive again. I crept out into the night and went back to Jill, who was sitting up in bed at Ashton's waiting for me.

She gave one look at my face.

"What happened? I hoped you'd be tight as a lord."

I couldn't bring myself to say anything at all beyond:

"One Survivor is going under. We've decided to go to his rescue."

"What's funny about that? It seems obvious."

Then her face tightened.

"Don't tell me it's you. . . . Don't tell me that you——"

"Don't worry," I said; "it's not me."

That was my last Survivors' Dinner. I'm still trying to tell you about the Odd Volumes.

After some genial banter and general introductions of our guests to His Oddship the President, Brother Arbalister (in private life

Kenneth Macrae Moir, solicitor), we followed His Oddship into the banqueting chamber and sat down some fifty or sixty strong.

The dinner opens with an amusing ritual, the bringing by the Master of Ceremonies (Russell Vick, the famous and handsome white-haired K.C.) of the body of the Key of the Archives on a velvet cushion. His Oddship raised the key in his right hand, and having pronounced (in the old-fashioned way) the brief grace, "*Incipit feliciter caena*," he said in English:

"The 567th meeting of the Sette of Odd Volumes is now open."

We immediately settled down to read first the menu, then the message from the Secretary on the opposite page, then the book of the Odd Volumes which gives the rules, names and addresses of all the members and a bibliography of the privately printed opusculae. The menu was a good one:

> *Le Tortue au Sherry en Tasse*
> *Le Filet de Sole Margnery*
> *Le Dindonneau Rôti Châtelaine*
> *Les Pommes Succès*
> *Le Petits pois fins*
> *L'Ananas voilé Sultane*
> *Les Friandises*
> *Le Café*

I always give my guests an innocuous Alsatian hock. Wealthier hosts plied their guests with champagne.

On the cover of the menu was a print of a man in a curious skull cap reading some documents. Under it ran the caption:

> An advocate in his study (*circa* 1833), or Brother
> Listener preparing his Paper!

On the inner side, facing the list of fare, was the Secretary's greeting to the guests, warning them of what was in store for them.

> You will be presented to His Oddship: you will be given a drink or six by your host . . . you will be entertained by our odd ceremonies, our ample board and our incomparable conversation,

and so on.

Conversation at Odd Volume dinners always flows easily. I compared it with the Survivors' Dinner when I had to rack my brain, quite ineffectively, to make small-talk with men who were boys when I was a boy.

Yet here I was surrounded by judges and barristers of great eminence, in whose presence I ought to be abashed, not only holding my own but enjoying myself.

Opposite to me sat Brother Scholemaster, whose guest was a young black-haired man who told me that he had been at Rossall, where I had been a master. He led me on to give my views on Rossall in particular, and public schools in general. I was, as I always am about education, pretty forceful and revolutionary.

I had let myself go for quite a quarter of an hour before I discovered that this youngster was the High Master of St. Paul's. I ought to have known, for it is the custom for Odd Volumes to bring guests even more distinguished than themselves. This adds a piquancy to the condescension with which they treat them in their introductory speeches. For when the dinner is over and the minutes have been read, each member of the Sette has to stand up and introduce his guests.

I remember taking Nelson Keys, who had a genius for imitating other people. Without letting him know beforehand I introduced him as Leslie Henson. He immediately became Leslie Henson, and quite a large part of the assembly thought that he really was Henson.

After the guests had been introduced we settled down to listen to the golden voice of Sir Norman Birkett (Brother Listener) as he read his paper on "Advocacy". It was by far the most brilliant paper that I have ever listened to since I joined the Sette. Earlier on in the evening I had registered a complaint.

"When Brother Listener," I said, "was President he asked me to give his year of office a propitious send-off. I took infinite pains to write a paper on a subject that escapes me for the moment, but it contained one immortal sentence which I do remember. It was this: 'Whether the ancient custom of paying a token rent with a red nose on St. John's Day still continues I am unable to ascertain.'

"Brother Listener elected to be ill on the night I read my paper which was dismissed by the Secretary as inaudible. At the following meeting Brother Spectator described tediously and at length a story of how he escaped from Pentonville in a jet-propelled aeroplane. As the Bishop said to Swift after reading *Gulliver's Travels*, I don't believe a word of it. Yet the Odd Council have honoured Brother Spectator by printing his unworthy opuscule. Mine lies neglected, unwept, unhonoured and unsung. I have a proposal to make. If

Brother Listener will pay for the printing of my paper, a copy of which I sent him to read, I will pay for the printing of his doubtless painfully puerile paper on Advocacy which I have yet to hear."

Brother Listener rose to his feet and said that as Brother Perambulator was without doubt the greatest writer the world had ever seen he gladly accepted his generous offer.

When at the end of the evening I went over to thank him for his inspired address he said:

"To speak seriously, Brother, I have long been trying to tell you that your autobiography was one of the most refreshing, most human and most moving pieces of self-revelation I have ever read. Do please let us have the other half."

"For you, Brother, I would do anything. I will even dedicate it to you."

As soon as I got back to Ashton's Hotel, where Jill was as usual sitting up waiting for me, she saw from my face that this was no repetition of the Survivors' Dinner.

"Well?" she said.

"Very well," I said. "I'm going to write the story of the second half of my life."

# CHAPTER II

## I· LUNCH ON THE EGGLI (1951)

I HAVEN'T invoked Jill's help in this fragmentary Autobiography because I don't want help. I want to reveal myself as I see myself, not as she or anybody else sees me, but I did ask her this question.

"What," I asked, "do you think my answer is to the question 'Which was the happiest moment of your life?'"

She replied instantly:

"When you were upside down in the snow on the Hornfluh after falling off the ski-hoist."

"It was our luncheon together outside the lonely hut on the Eggli."

"Mine was our luncheon outside the anything but lonely hotel on the Scheidegg."

"There," I said, "lies the difference between us. You like people. I like solitude, the mountains to myself."

Why was that the happiest moment or hour of my life? Because it was in the sun in the snow on the top of a mountain and shared with Jill and Imogen. There were also sizzling bacon and eggs, a carafe of Swiss wine, and the society of a young Swiss mountaineer.

I was completely carefree, completely happy, on top of the world in every sense.

I don't want to keep dwelling on the dreary topic of my illness, but in order that you may understand why this moment on the Eggli stands out as a red-letter moment you must remember that for six months before I was of no more use to the world than I was to myself. I was down and out physically, mentally and financially.

I stayed in bed till eleven or twelve, sank on to the settee in my study and went straight to sleep again. Jill commented on the fact that my appetite was still good, and, hanging on that single fact, tried to bully me back to action. I occasionally, for her sake, dragged myself to the flicks and found them only bearable when I shut my eyes and went to sleep.

My only comfort was gin, and I drank precious little of that. I couldn't afford more than a glass a day.

I couldn't even follow the stories of the novels I was being paid to review in the *Oxford Mail*. If anybody came to the house I shut myself in my study and refused to come out till they had gone.

I couldn't even rouse myself to make the necessary arrangements to go to Switzerland.

It so happened that when we did go (on 23rd December) we had the worst journey that I can remember. We had paid beforehand for dinner on the French train and breakfast on the Swiss train. It was only by a miracle that we secured luncheon on the boat-train to Folkestone.

We ate that at 12 noon on the Friday. No food or drink passed our lips till two o'clock on the Saturday afternoon.

The cross-channel steamer was so overcrowded that having secured a seat in a howling draught we had no alternative but to stay put. Jill contracted a chill which she didn't shake off for over a fortnight.

On the train at Calais we found that we had to share an extremely uncomfortable compartment with five other people. In other words, eight of us had to sit wedged close together right through the night. We were told that our dinner was the third service and would be served at ten o'clock.

With a great effort we climbed over and past hordes of French people who occupied all the corridors, and having fought our way along the whole length of the train we found that the lock of the door connecting the dining-car and the rest of the train was broken, with the result that those who had dined couldn't get back to their compartments, and those like ourselves, who had left their compartments in order to dine, couldn't get into the dining-car.

We arrived at Basle an hour late, to find that the train to Interlaken, containing the breakfast-car, had gone. We followed in a slow train, nearly fainting with exhaustion and hunger. We had brought nothing to eat or drink. At Interlaken we made a bee-line for the Hotel du Lac and were restored to life by a luncheon that cost £2 10s. for the three of us.

When we arrived in Wengen it was raining. There was no one about. I wished that I had never come. I wished that I were dead. Yet here we were some fourteen days later sitting out in the sun in snow on the top of the Eggli in our shirtsleeves, happier than sandboys.

What had happened? How can I account for it? I can't account for it. I can only say that it is possible to go down into Hell and climb out again into Heaven.

My financial condition had not changed. I had entirely forgotten my financial condition. I had forgotten my mental depression, and certainly overcome my physical lethargy.

I was out on skis on the nursery slopes every sunny hour of every sunny day and I was completely transformed. It wasn't that I was ski-ing well. I was ski-ing worse than I have ever skied in my life. I had indeed achieved the rare distinction of falling off the ski-hoist just below the summit of the Hornfluh, and, nearly suffocated in the snow with my skis sticking up in the air, had reduced Imogen and Jill to such hysterical laughter that I lost my temper and sulked for hours.

I had been told not only by the English but by the Swiss that no man in his senses skies after fifty. I've told you my age, sixty-five. I wasn't even insured against accidents.

I skied all day, I drank Gluhwein when the sun went down, and without any success at all tried to keep Jill from buying absurd souvenirs.

Every night, fortified by a bottle of Spiezer, I danced with Jill and Imogen from nine till midnight. I even allowed Jill to teach me the Samba.

I had the sun in the morning and the moon flooding the snow-clad Alps at night.

I was indeed all right.

Well, there you are. If you feel that you are about to enter a mental home try Switzerland first.

I was trying to tell you why this picnic on the top of the Eggli was the happiest hour of my life. In the first place I had escaped from death to life, from an apparently unending tunnel into the light of day. I was lightheaded with happiness.

I had just been very badly frightened. A sledge-hoist sounds innocent. We arrived at the funicular station entirely unsuspecting what lay in store for us.

We climbed into the rickety old sledge and long before I was ready we had started. I hadn't realized that we were to climb up the face of a house. I daren't look down into the depths below. I daren't look up at the heights above. I looked, and kept my eyes fixed, on the deep snow at my side.

"If the cable breaks we shall go with a bit of a bang," said Imogen cheerfully. I could have lynched her.

"I think I'd rather have the s-s-s-ski-h-h-hoist," I stammered. My teeth had nearly chattered themselves out of my mouth.

"Don't you like it?" asked Jill.

" 'Like' is inadequate to express what I feel," I replied. "I'll tell you if we ever reach the top."

"Oh, the top's more than five thousand feet above this," said Imogen.

"In that case," I said, "we shall be in this contraption for half an hour at least. They ought to provide overcoats."

"And side curtains and soft cushions and hassocks," added Imogen. "There's no satisfying you, Daddy. I wonder you don't complain because there isn't a dining-car."

"I'm not hungry," I said. "Is there any brandy in the house?"

"In your hip-pocket," said Jill, "where it always is."

"As I daren't lift a finger in any direction," I said, "it'll have to stay there."

"It's the first time I've ever known you refusing drink when it was available," said Jill.

"That's just it. It isn't available."

In spite of the cold I was sweating profusely when at last we reached the summit.

Imogen looked down, a thing I dared not do.

"Quite a hill," she said.

"I'm walking down," I said.

"There's no path," she said. "You'd sink in the snow."

"We ought to have brought our skis."

Jill laughed a little cynically.

"I'd give a lot to see you ski-ing on these slopes."

"Perhaps if I rolled," I urged.

"You'd be quite a snowball by the time you reached the bottom," said Imogen.

Our fellow passengers were few, all male, all Swiss, and all so sombrely dressed that I knew that they must be experts.

I watched them bind on their skis, throw their arms into the air with cries of delight and disappear over the edge of the precipice with the ease and grace of seagulls leaving a rock face.

We turned to face a land of virgin snow, completely deserted. The silence was absolute. There was a red board on which was written "Restaurant: 15 minutes." A finger-post pointed over the white slopes.

"Poleward Ho!" I shouted and strode ahead. I didn't stride ahead long. I found myself sinking into the deep soft snow.

Well over twenty minutes later, sweating profusely, I looked down from the summit of a little peak to a black-gabled chalet hidden in a hollow. An Alsatian dog lying in the sun in front of the door saw me and barked angrily.

"They don't get many visitors," said Jill.

"Thank God," I said. "Perhaps we can get a cup of milk."

A very old man came out to greet us as we drew nearer.

There were half a dozen well-scoured tables in front of the house, and more tables behind glass. He had no English. I didn't know the German for milk, so I shouted "Chocolat" several times. He seemed to understand. I held up three fingers. He seemed to understand that too.

"It's marvellous how well Daddy makes himself understood," said Imogen.

"So long as he never opens his mouth," said Jill. "I like this place."

She wandered away into the distance with the camera. She fell in some unusually deep soft snow. That made me very happy. She usually picks her way with care.

I looked round at the mighty peaks, the vast mass of the Rutli, the jagged peak of the Gumfluh. We looked across the five valleys to the fastnesses above, the National Game Preserve of the Grimmer. I looked through my field-glasses for chamois. There were no chamois or ibex. On the lower slopes were black trees, but our world, the upper world, was just one great sea of pure white. I looked up to the Pass of Collon, where no traffic can pass till the Spring sun melts the snow. I could not name one of the peaks that enclosed the horizon of my new world. I didn't want to. An old man and woman in Victorian clothes suddenly emerged from nowhere with skins on their skis. So they had climbed, as all good men and true had to before the invention of sledge-hoists, ski-hoists, funiculars and cable-cars. I could have kissed them both as they waxed their skis and hung them up in front of the hut to dry.

Then a wizened little old lady carrying a marketing bag skied gracefully down the slopes to the hut and disappeared inside.

A little later a handsome black-haired Swiss boy, accompanied by an attractive young blonde, also skied in and sat down at the next table. The girl found a deck-chair, lay back in it, and went to sleep. The Swiss boy went inside the hut to order something.

I just gazed and gazed. Nobody spoke. The silence was so lovely that I didn't want it to be broken, ever.

The little old woman reappeared, carrying coffee on a tray with a bottle of Kirsch in her other hand.

"Heavens!" I shouted, "can you get drinks here?"

The Swiss boy seemed to be amused.

"Why not?" he said.

I rubbed my eyes.

"I forgot. I'm English. Only in prohibited areas in the Highlands of Scotland can you get privately distilled whiskey, and then they cut your head off if you're caught. It's nice to be civilized. Would you prevail upon her to leave that bottle of Kirsch on this table?"

"Sure," said the Swiss boy.

I didn't reply "O.K.", which seemed the appropriate answer.

He then began a conversation with the old woman which threatened to last till sundown.

"It takes a long time in your language to say 'Put down the bottle,'" I said.

"Sure," he said.

The old woman passed with a plate of sizzling soup.

"Look," I said. "Something to eat as well."

"What would you like?" asked the Swiss boy.

Imogen looked at me warningly.

"We've paid for our lunch in the hotel," she said. "We ought to go."

I disregarded, as I always do, my youngest daughter's attempt to keep her father on the straight and narrow path.

"Primroses for me," I said.

The Swiss boy for once didn't say "Sure." He looked puzzled.

"Sorry," I said. "I meant bacon and eggs."

His face lightened.

"Sure," he said.

This was fairyland indeed.

The wizened woman was called and obviously agreed that bacon and eggs were not only possible but would be with us in a twinkling.

I began my strip-tease act. I was too hot. I divested myself of my duffle coat, two scarves, green ski-ing tunic, black thick woollen jersey, my yellow hunting waistcoat, my under-waistcoat, and arriving at last at my pure white silk shirt, rolled up my sleeves.

I thought the Swiss boy was going to ask for my autograph. He obviously thought better of it and said quietly:

"Too hot?"

"I was," I said.

"Sure," he replied.

I had no idea that he was a member of our party. Perhaps he thought that I really was going to walk down.

"See you at the bottom," he said cryptically.

"Bottom?" I repeated. "Bottom of what?"

He had already put on his skis with something of the ease with which I put on my pyjamas and disappeared over the horizon.

"Pegasus," I said.

"Pegasus," said Imogen severely, "was a horse."

I stumbled a good deal over the snow getting back to the sledge-hoist.

Luckily I had the support of the blonde to whom the Swiss boy had addressed no word. She had, wisely, I think, slept through the golden day. I felt on top of the world. I told her so.

I think her answer was:

"Excuse."

"Sure," I said. "And 'pardon' to you."

It's a most curious thing, but I enjoyed the descent in the sledge. It was with some difficulty that Imogen kept me in my seat.

"You know," I said, "it'd be rather fun to roll down. I bet you a centime that I'd race you. Come on, be a sport."

"Really," said Jill, "there are times."

"Times!" I said. "Sure there are times. Hullo! Why have we stopped?"

"It's usual to stop at the end of a journey," said Imogen.

I looked round on the flat land before me. I had descended from the Mount of Transfiguration.

"The happiest day, the happiest day of my life," I said. "I wonder if there's anywhere we could get a drink."

"We're still in Switzerland," said Jill.

# CHAPTER III

## I Bury My Mother (1939)

My mother died on 7th March, 1939. She was the first person I ever saw die, and I suppose she was closer to me in several ways than any other person I had known or ever should know.

She was a character and I adored her. She led my father, who was patient to the point of dumbness, a trying life. She could hardly bear to let him out of her sight, and she used to sit for hours in the bow-window of the drawing-room looking across the valley to the Matlock Road for a sign of his lights if he was in a car or on his bicycle.

What she was afraid of I never discovered. She disliked children with a thoroughness that was characteristic of all her likes and dislikes.

She liked peers of the realm, and was never tired of reminding us of her connexion with the Petre family. Her mother was a Petre. There I have inherited something. I too like being on nodding terms with lords. At Christ Church I was able to indulge that fancy.

Both my father and mother were poor. His income as Rector was under £300 a year. My mother had saved a little from the wreck when her farmer brother ran through £40,000 breeding pedigree beasts and giving champagne parties. She juggled with this minute legacy so effectively that after her death I found to my surprise that I was £4,000 or £5,000 richer. She had a secret vice that neither I nor my father ever suspected. She kept a notebook in which she jotted down all the changes in the prices of stocks and shares, and she spent the greater part of her life not, as I thought, in reading good books, but in buying and selling stocks and shares. It is odd to think of a country parson's wife having a flair for investments, but when I tell you that I am only able to carry on because of her perspicacity about I.C.I. and certain breweries you will agree that she had character. If you must gamble, the Stock Exchange is more profitable than football pools or horses.

In spite of the fact that she was terrified of almost everything in life (thunder invariably drove her to a cupboard under the stairs) she enjoyed it.

She enjoyed cooking. She was a superb cook. She enjoyed eating and drinking and wearing expensive clothes (her only extravagance). She enjoyed sitting on the free seats (rather than pay twopence for a deck chair she would stand menacingly above the full free benches for hours) on the Promenade at Brighton, Southport and Weston-super-Mare. The fact that these were her favourite resorts shows that she was gregarious.

I don't remember a single instance in the whole of their lives when my father and mother took a cab or taxi. On the contrary I have the most vivid memories of walking up and down the Front at Blackpool and Bournemouth carrying heavy suitcases and calling in at one boarding-house after another in search of the cheapest. Never did it occur to them to write to any place beforehand to secure rooms.

They had guts, those strange parents of mine. We lived in a rather tough village, the inhabitants of which worked either in the cotton mills below the Rectory or in the quarries on the hill above. These Derbyshire folk are people of independent spirit and their natural bias is against the Established Church and strongly in favour of some form of Nonconformity. The Methodist, Wesleyan and Baptist Chapels flourished. The Church was in eclipse.

My mother had the notion that she was a sort of Squire's wife, and though she took little part in Parish life she expected all the labourers to touch their caps to her and the mill-girls to curtsey.

As in appearance she closely resembled Queen Victoria and in demeanour the Duchess of Wrexe, she (*mirabile dictu!*) succeeded to some extent in eliciting these acknowledgments of her social superiority. The villagers found that it paid. The Wesleyan minister was rewarded for touching his cap by being given odd jobs in the garden which, like most rectory gardens, was about the size of a public park.

Both my parents were enthusiastic gardeners, which was lucky for me because the easiest money I ever earned was the tuppence that I got for bringing in buckets of horse-manure from the road at the top of the drive. I was pretty quick off the mark then and would stand just inside the main gate waiting for the appearance of the drays coming down from the stone quarries or the milk cart or the grocer's van. I was out like a flash when any horse functioned, as I earnestly prayed to God that he would, just outside the gates so that I should be first in the field. Tuppence was a lot of money then and in my early childhood I had a passion for literature. Even today the sight of a copy of *Ally Sloper* turns my head. My mother was an equally passionate addict of books, but not of reading. Her only gauge of a book's quality was by smelling it. If it smelt as if it had come straight from the printer she would treasure it. If it was not a mint copy she would hold it at arm's length, owing to the risk she stood in of contagion and infection by reason of its germs.

She stood in daily terror of every disease there was.

There had been in the sixties an outbreak of cholera in Gloucester. She had to pass through Gloucester in the train in order to reach her Devon home which she revisited every other year. I can see her now, taking out her heavily scented handkerchief (she always smelt lovely) as the train stopped. "Brodie," she would say to my father, and to me, "Stuart" (I was known to her but to nobody else as Stuart), and in obedience to her we would produce our handkerchiefs.

"Don't breathe," she would say, "don't breathe again until we are well on the other side of Gloucester."

So all-compelling was my mother's influence that I never hear the word Gloucester without thinking of cholera.

As a child I seem to have lived in a world that smelt of camphor. Like all superstitious people, my mother had a blind faith in all remedies. I certainly inherited my passion for hoarding medicine-bottles from her.

I can't remember her suffering from any illness until she became the victim of arthritis.

I can remember offering to read to her in bed, and after an hour of Cowper's letters she raised a weary head and said: "On the whole I'd prefer to die in my own way. The fellow's mad, quite mad."

Her criticisms and opinions of literary giants were all her own. I remember her saying to me once: "You never listen to anything I say or take any advice that I give you, but I implore you to remember this one thing. Pray to God day and night that you don't become a second Shelley." There was little danger of that.

My mother was an open book for all men to read: intolerant, autocratic, intensely amusing, fantastically nervous, snobbish, and hypochondriacal. My father was an enigma. I have no idea what kind of a man he was. He was completely under my mother's thumb either because he was too lazy to rebel or because she was in control of the purse.

He seldom composed a sermon during the whole fifty-two years that he held the living. He used to read the sermons of 17th-century divines, most of them far above the heads of the handful of cottagers who attended church. He reminded me of Tommy Strong, Dean of "The House", who, as Bishop of Oxford, addressed the confirmees at Radley thus:

"Those of you who are well versed in comparative theology and those of you who are less well versed will agree with me that . . ."

My father was extraordinarily absent-minded, and seemed never really to have any real contact with the passing world.

On the day that I first ran for Oxford against Cambridge he was present at an Archidiaconal conference.

The Bishop of Southwell congratulated him on the fact.

My father blinked and said:

"Ah, yes, yes, my Lord, but I think you have made a mistake. I have a son, but I rather think that he is at Cambridge."

As my father was himself an athlete, a Rowing Blue, this makes the story even more difficult to believe.

As I have said, he was an enigma. Like Thomas Gray, he never spoke out. From the beginning of my life to the end of his, he never gave me a single piece of advice about anything.

He was taciturn, but by no means saturnine. He laughed a good deal. He laughed more than he spoke. He could—and in later life did—often get angry.

He never vented his anger on me until after my mother's death, when he once turned on me like an adder for remonstrating with him about his habit of crossing the road in his car without warning. The first occasion on which I saw him lose his temper was on the Rectory lawn, when he had allowed a passing knife-grinder to sharpen the lawn-mower. Unluckily for him the grinder waited to see my father test it.

"Blast and damn you to hell!" suddenly said my father. "You've ruined the blasted thing."

I burst into tears and waited for God to strike him dead for blasphemy. This outburst was all the more strange because my father did not swear. I have no idea whether he was a happy man or not. He disliked his own father so much that in spite of being his eldest son he refused to go to his funeral. This may have been partly because of my mother's refusal to acknowledge the existence of any of the Mais family.

I adored my paternal grandfather, who lived to be ninety-six, but I can well see why his own sons and daughters were less well-disposed towards him. He never did a day's work in his life. He ran through his own and my grandmother's fortune. He bullied my grandmother, who was one of the outstanding beauties of her day, so much that she spent most of her days in tears and died when she was still relatively young.

He was a man of quite ungovernable temper.

I remember one day after morning prayers, which all the staff had to attend as well as the family, he rose to his great bearded height and shouted:

"Who laid this table?"

One trembling maid came forward.

"That salt-cellar," he shouted, "is not in place."

He gave the tablecloth a tug and pulled everything on the table —plates, cups, pots of coffee and tea, eggs and sausages—on to the floor. I could have hugged him.

He used to drive a high dogcart, and for the sheer devil of it lash out with his long riding-whip at all the villagers who stood in the street to see him pass by. I can vouch for the truth of that because the blacksmith in Georgeham showed me a lasting memento that he had received from my grandfather's whip. He didn't bear the old man a grudge.

There were certainly characters on both sides of my family. My mother's brother, who earned her lasting hatred for running through the family money and going bankrupt (he emigrated to Tasmania), was one of my boyhood heroes. He had two farms some sixteen miles apart and he used to drive from one to the other in a dogcart. I was his only nephew and he had taken a fancy to me, so he would rescue me from my maiden aunts at Yarde, pack me into the dogcart by his side, and go straight off to sleep, leaving the horse to take him home. The Devon lanes are high-banked and narrow. It was as well that he lived before the days of cars.

He enchanted me by his behaviour in his own farm of Boode, Braunton. I can't remember whether he drank champagne for luncheon regularly, but I do remember how delighted I used to be when he took up empty champagne bottle after empty champagne bottle and hurled them one after another through the large dining-room window on to the lawn outside. I remember this lawn contained more broken glass than grass because we used to try to play tennis on it.

Really I don't think there was much to choose in oddity between the Mais family and the Petre Tamlyn family. Both were extremely wealthy at the time that my father married my mother. Both families had lost all their money by the time that I had grown up. My mother's brother Horden was more generous than my father's father. Horden gave his money away. How my paternal grandfather ran through his fortune I don't know.

I should say that the Mais side were the less respectable. In the late 18th or early 19th century my great-great-grandfather, who was a West Indian sugar merchant in Bristol, eloped with his children's governess to Guernsey and, having started an illegitimate family there, deserted her and went off to Jamaica to raise a coloured family there. The name of Mais is well known in the West Indies. I have met one or two coloured Maises who have come up to Oxford as Rhodes scholars. They were much finer physically than I was. There is some disadvantage in being the eldest son of an eldest son of an eldest son.

I am not passionately excited about pedigrees, but I had an uncle Mais who went to immense pains to see how far back he could trace the family. We never seem to have achieved any fame in any direction with the exception of my great-grandfather, who introduced Rugby football into Australia. I am told that we go back to Saxon times, but Mais doesn't sound to me Saxon. I am inclined to think that the word is of Dutch origin. All I know is that we have been in the country a long time.

The Petres are in a quite different category. I've got pedigrees of my mother's family going back to Richard II. The Hordens go back to Saxon days. The word Horden is a variant of Haldane, i.e. Half-Dane.

Some of the Petres have been comparatively eminent. Sir William Petre, who was educated at Exeter College, Oxford, became a Privy Councillor under Henry VIII, a Principal Secretary of State under Edward VI and Chancellor of the Order of the Garter under Bloody Mary. He was also one of Queen Elizabeth's councillors. His son was created Baron Petre of Writtle, in Essex. Another member of the family, Hugh Petre, was Oliver Cromwell's chaplain, and he had to use his influence to secure the release of Thomas Petre of Harlyn, who had been taken prisoner while fighting for Charles I. It was Thomas Petre who restored the family mansion of Harlyn, which is a most sinister, haunted house near Constantine in Cornwall.

No wonder my mother was superstitious. There is a story of Mrs. Mary Withel, who was by birth a Petre, hearing the footsteps of her brother John Petre in the passage of her Padstow house. As she called to him to come to the kitchen she heard a heavy fall, and she rushed out to find the passage empty. An hour later a messenger from Trenean, her brother's house, came to announce that John had been accidentally shot an hour before.

Early in the 17th century one of the Petres was killed by a fall from his horse. Just before the accident his portrait fell from a wall and damaged that part of the face where he afterwards received the fatal injury. My own cousin Charles Petre Lovell, an undergraduate of St. John's College, Oxford, was drowned after his canoe had capsized owing to his dog jumping overboard. He was only twenty-two.

No Charles Petre has ever lived to be twenty-three.

The most famous member of my family was Admiral Robert Blake.

If facial resemblance means anything I haven't much Petre blood in me, because I have a portrait of an 18th-century Lord Petre whose high arched nose is the only feature that we have in common.

On the other hand there is a portrait in Coughton Court, Warwickshire, the seat of the Throckmortons, of Sir Charles Throckmorton, who was born in 1757 and died in 1840, which is so exactly like me both in nose, eyes, crooked mouth, chin and, most of all, hands, that everyone who has seen it agrees that he must be an ancestor of mine. The Throckmortons, in fact, intermarried with the Petres. Both are ancient Catholic families.

I wish that my mother could have lived to have seen that portrait.

I do not wish her to have lived longer for any other reason. She would have found little pleasure in a war that brought bombs and rationing to our quiet Derbyshire village.

My mother never forgave me for describing her as sprung from farming stock. I am as much of a snob as she and proud of it. I have no sympathy whatever with the aims of those people who see evil in the caste system. I am a member of what was once the ruling class, and I am glad about that. I am proud of my Petre ancestry in spite of the fact that they haven't done much through the centuries. But why it is a good thing to be a lord and a shameful thing to be a farmer I can't see. I know several lords who are farmers. It seems the obvious thing for a lord to be. If the land is his why not develop it? I know that my mother lived in a peculiarly illogical time. We called on the doctor, but not on the dentist.

I recall the housemaster's wife at Sherborne who, in reply to my statement that I was proud to live in the same county as Thomas Hardy, said, "Mr. Hardy isn't a gentleman."

I would rather speak the English of Christopher Stone than that of some of our Cabinet Ministers. I would rather be of gentle birth than of lowly birth. I realize that it is an accident, and I am not being superior when I claim to be gently born.

I naturally applaud anyone who has the guts to rise out of the ruck, but I see nothing praiseworthy in claiming to belong to the rank and file.

The trouble with "the common people", a favourite phrase of my mother's, is that they are just that. They are common. They are as common as starlings. There are too many of them. They occupy seats to the exclusion of the uncommon who are being eliminated to the country's great loss. England's greatness was not built by the common people but by the uncommon people, by Elizabeth, Raleigh, Cromwell, Marlborough, and Blake. Jill is rightly proud of her German and Irish ancestry. She is a Schiller.

There is a bastard snobbery that I really hate, that of the lord who affects to despise his title. If you're Winston Churchill, plain Mr. is good enough. There is no title that would be adequate recognition for the services he has done the State. The rest of us may well be gratified with any crumb of recognition that falls to us. I should be as pleased as Punch if for some extraordinary reason I saw myself honoured with a knighthood in the Birthday Honours.

I always feel self-important when I find myself introducing Lalage or Imogen to a lord. Imogen is not impressionable, but Lalage turns on her best quality charm when I produce a member of the Aristocracy. That is as it should be. The best people should bring out the best in us; just as in church we give free play to the holy side of us which gets so little chance to make itself felt outside church.

My mother was certainly a snob in her relations with the Almighty. She put on a special voice when she addressed Him as "Gawd". I should say that she was much more godly than my father.

My mother, as I said, died in 1939, and my father followed her to the grave a few years later.

My father has become a shadow. My mother haunts me, and is still very much alive. "How Mutts" (our nickname for her), says Jill, "would have adored that," "How Mutts would have loathed this."

Her forceful character is still about my path and about my bed.

# CHAPTER IV

## Last Days at Toad Hall (1937-40)

My friends express surprise on learning that I usually start work about three o'clock in the morning, and my doctor suggests darkly that my end will be sudden and sticky.

> I burn my candle at both ends,
>   It will not last the night;
> But ah, my foes, and oh, my friends—
>   It gives a lovely light.

Let me tell you about this lovely light.

I keep on my desk a Commando knife, a Highland dagger and a miniature Spanish rapier as used by the matadors. When passing lorry-drivers see the light in my windows they occasionally stop in the hope of a cup of tea. I make three lots of tea between three o'clock and breakfast, but I dislike sharing my cheering cup with doubtful characters.

Usually it is enough for them to approach the window. They may not even see the knives. What they see is quite enough.

Almost invariably they think better of it and don't tap at the window. To those who, greatly daring, tap, I hold up my knives. On sight of these their thirst usually deserts them and they disappear quickly and silently into the blackness of the night.

I work hard and fast through the dark hours, happy in the thought that I cannot be disturbed by telephone or family.

You may judge therefore of my surprise when one morning, it must have been about four o'clock, I looked round to see on the settee, looking pensively into the fire, a prepossessing young girl. Her hair was the colour of honey, her cheeks pink and white, her legs long and slender. Everything about her was charming. She looked exactly like Jill at seventeen.

Not wishing to frighten her I said quietly:

"The Lord be with you."

To which she replied:

"And with Blithe Spirit."

"What?" I said.

She repeated the sentence.

"That's what I thought you said. Have a cup of tea."

"I'd rather have gin."

"As you wish. I don't usually drink gin at this hour in the morning."

"If you were going to bed instead of getting up you would."

"There's a world of difference. Pink or French?"

"Italian."

"I like a girl who knows her own mind. How old are you?"

"How old would you say?"

"Seventeen."

"You'd be right. A woman is as old as she appears to a man."

I handed her the gin. She drank it at a gulp and handed me the glass.

"May I?" she asked. "I've come rather a long way."

"Of course. Why?"

"Why what?"

"Why have you come a long way?"

"To see you, of course."

"Of course."

It seemed impolite to ask how she got in. Lalage has a habit of coming in from her dances about three o'clock and often leaves the door unlocked. I presumed that this was one of her associates, though I should have expected her escort to be a young man.

"I'm honoured," I added.

"I thought you would be." She looked round the room. "How long have you had this house?"

For once I didn't resent the intrusion. I welcomed it. I put down my pen.

"Is this an interview?"

She smiled. Her smile lit up her face. It was then that I saw that her eyes were also just like Jill's.

"You don't mind?"

"On the contrary."

"How long have you had this house?"

"That's a funny place to start," I said.

"Not at all. I've read *All the Days of My Life*. That takes us up to 1937. What happened then?"

I offered her my snuff-box.

"I'd rather have a cigarette."

"There's a box by your side."

As I lit her cigarette for her I took a closer look.

"Forgive my saying so. You rather dazzle me. You're exactly like Jill."

"I'm not going to cover my face on that account."

I breathed more easily.

For a split second I had an uncanny feeling that . . . She was laughing easily.

"No. I didn't die before the God of Love was born."

"That's a comfort, anyway. It only struck me that you were——"

"Were what?"

"I can't get the exact word. Tenuous."

"Is it a crime to be insubstantial?"

"I didn't say insubstantial. Anyway, I like you the way you are. Please stay that way."

"That at any rate I can promise. We're not getting on very fast, are we?"

"I feel that I've known you all my life."

"Would it surprise you if you had?"

"Don't let's get metaphysical. It's enough for me that you are here now."

"We've got as far as 1937," she said. "Here's to the next fourteen years."

"How did you know that I was writing my Autobiography?"

"You'd be silly if you didn't. You've such a lot to say. What it feels like to have been world famous and then——"

"Then merely M-A-I-S—S for Sugar."

She laughed again.

"I think that's rather funny, Humpty-Dumpty."

"Humpty-Dumpty didn't think so."

"There's no evidence either way. I want to restore your self-esteem."

"Well, if you want to know, I'm feeling much more like my old self since you came in."

"Then my journey was worth while. About 1937."

I had to think.

"I've forgotten. I'll have to look at my ledger."

"I didn't know you kept accounts."

"Only of the cheques that come in for income-tax purposes."

I went to the drawer where I keep my bills, receipts, bank-books and all things connected with my finances.

"I've lost my old book," I said. "This one begins on 17th September, 1937."

"That's good enough," she said.

"We were living in Toad Hall then," I said, and was suddenly overcome with nostalgia. "There was the village green, cricket, sun, the sea, bathing. Lalage was six, Imogen a year old. Life was very heaven. I was on top of the world."

"Were you? Didn't you keep a diary?"

"I did. It's on the shelf there."

"Take it down and have a look at it."

"It doesn't begin till 1st November," I said, and began to read, aloud:

" 'In the middle of the morning while Jill was rearranging the furniture in my study (her favourite occupation) . . .' " I stopped reading. "It still is. She's always rearranging the furniture."

"Never mind that. Go on reading." I read on.

" 'While Jill was rearranging the furniture in my study and I was trying to get the characters in my new novel to come alive the telephone bell rang. It was a solicitor. I had apparently written something about a playwright to which he had taken exception. He wants £500 damages or a public apology.' "

"Just flick over a few pages, and you'll see whether that was the Golden Age or if it only seems so at this distance of time."

I skimmed over the pages lightly. My eye caught the phrase "Lalage in a tantrum". There was some trouble with the bank. Advertising firms had commissioned work and then cancelled it.

I looked up.

"I was at any rate broadcasting a lot."

"Yes. There was that. You're missing that."

"More than I can say."

I turned over the pages.

"I was hunting on foot with the Crawley. I miss that too."

"There are usually compensations. Oxford has something."

"We'll come to that when I get there. We played tennis a lot. We never play now."

I turned one more page.

"I was lecturing all over the country. No one asks me to lecture now. I was taking ramblers out every Sunday over the South Downs. I got a lot of money for that."

"Is money everything?"

"When you haven't got any, yes. Here's an account of our

ment just because a bully looked like biting us. Something seemed to come over England that Summer. I went on broadcasting but we'd stopped laughing. The air was tense. Life had become a bad dream. Something had gone out of it. We had found that we hadn't the guts we thought we had. Then Priscilla married her French vicomte. There was another Southwick cricket dinner. In January 1939 I was asked to stand as Liberal candidate for Cirencester and Tewkesbury. I felt honoured but refused. Sir Henry Lunn asked us to go on a cruise to the West Indies free of charge. I was honoured but refused. I did more walking for the Southern Railway. We had decided to go to Egypt and round the Mediterranean, but my mother fell ill. She died on 7th March, 1939. She just missed the war. She was lucky."

"You loved your mother?"

"I adored her. I remember walking over the Quantock Hills. I insured my life for the last time. I was fifty-four. My mother left me about £5,000. We went back in August to Woolacombe and on 4th September my world died on me. We were, at last, at war. It's taking me a long time to get to Oxford."

"I'm in no hurry." She stretched out her arms and went back to the settee. I prayed for the dawn never to break. I enjoyed talking about myself to this attractive young girl. She seemed interested. She was playing Desdemona to my Othello. But I didn't call her Desdemona. I called her Penelope. She spent some of the time knitting, Jill's favourite occupation, but most of it unpicking what she had earlier knitted. I didn't ask her why.

"Yes," I went on, "the war caught us at Woolacombe. For me, it meant ruin. That year had been my peak year. One way and another I had raked in about £3,500.

"In a single day I was reduced to nothing, with very heavy commitments. It wasn't funny. What was funny (not funny 'ha-ha', but funny 'queer') was that practically everybody else of my standing switched over almost automatically to some paying job, in the Army, Navy and R.A.F. or one of the new Ministries. I was promised the earth and got nothing, and by nothing I mean nothing. I've never got back. That was twelve years ago."

"You must have done something."

"I offered myself as coast watcher. They wouldn't have me. There was nothing in the Services. I was too old, at fifty-four, to fight, or so they said when I applied. I was apparently also too old at fifty-four for any of the Ministries. It was the hell of a business."

"But, surely, the B.B.C.?"

"I'll tell you about that another night. A few scraps fell my way from their table. No. I went back to teaching."

"Tell me."

"Another night. I want to get on to Oxford."

"Have it your own way."

"The school was in Devon. That job lasted just eight weeks."

"Sacked?"

"For a change, no. We went back to Sussex on the 6th of November."

"And glad?"

"I'll say we were glad. Even if I hadn't got a job, I was Mr. Toad of Toad Hall again, among my own books, with room to move about. It seemed incredibly rich. We vowed that nothing would ever make us move again. Jill made me swear that we'd stay put however much we were bombed. I swore. We hadn't had any bombs then. I joined the Home Guard, L.D.V. we were called then, and defended the Downs at the back of the house with an old Service rifle."

I happened to look across the room at that moment and laughed.

"Come again," she said.

"That's just it," I said. "You're exactly like her."

"Who?"

"Don't you remember? 'She'd come again, and with a greedy ear devour up my discourse!' "

"Oh! Desdemona. You're not much like Othello. In face, I mean. Probably you'd be just as jealous."

"I don't think you'd ever give me cause."

"Desdemona didn't."

"Yes," I said, "I think you'd be just as faithful. But you're far lovelier. I like the way your hair curls round the nape of your neck."

"Thank you. That's what I like to hear you say. But hadn't we better get back to Sussex?"

I returned to my story.

"Those were the days of the phoney war. I wasn't incurring any of the dangers that Othello incurred. The only moving accident that came my way was being shot at in the dark by one of my own men."

"You make it sound as if you were often being shot at."

"On the contrary. Only twice before that. Once in a train in

E

America, between Chicago and Schenectady. I was playing chess with Jill at the time. Somebody in the snow outside took a pot-shot at us. It hit Jill's queen. The other was on my way back to Cranwell from the Air Ministry where I had been lecturing. This was at two o'clock in the morning and I was driving from Grantham station. Somebody ran out from the cover of the wood and plugged away at us for quite a time. Probably an Irishman. It was in the Sinn Fein days."

"You do live a gay life."

"I've had my moments. December 1939 wasn't one of them. I wrote letters to the headmistresses of girls' schools in England asking if I might lecture to them. I got one reply to every fifty letters I sent out. I remember one odd thing, Imogen's delight in shuffling through dead leaves. I've never met a child who gets more fun out of little things than she does. I hunted on foot with the Crawley. That was fun. I played tennis with Jill. That was fun because we're just about as good as each other."

"Weren't you writing anything?"

"I wrote a quite good short story about a fox and broadcast it. I was writing a spy novel and the diary of a citizen in war-time. I lectured to some nurses. We had our usual village cricket dinner. That cost me about £20."

"Extravagant man."

"I always got a tremendous kick out of it. Some of the B.B.C. high-ups used to come down. I broadcast from Evesham again. A long way for a fifteen-minute talk. I had to be away from home two days for that. So ended 1939. A very odd year.

"1940 started badly. Jill and I went up to Derbyshire to see my father and were nearly killed. He drove us on ice-bound roads to a lecture that I was giving in Barnsley. The car skidded and stopped within about an inch of the brink of a steep bank above a river.

"I did some 'Microphone At Large' feature programmes in the Midlands. We went up to Wellow, where we interviewed a first-rate blacksmith, and then came south to Fairford, where we found two magnificent farmers. From there we went to the Wyre Forest, where we broadcast an old man of ninety-eight who died the next morning. I remember getting a letter from Lalage in which she wrote: 'Imogen is carrying her gas-mask because she likes it so much.' I told you that Imogen has a flair for enjoyment.

"I then went to London to broadcast *The Thirty-nine Steps*, *Ivanhoe*, *Robinson Crusoe* and other books to schools. I began writing another spy novel. Both the children ran temperatures. It was a vilely cold winter. Then came one of those sudden changes that make England so lovely, the dawn chorus of birds, one of the loveliest things in the world."

"Which reminds me," said Penelope, looking up from her knitting anxiously.

"Heaps of time," I said. "We haven't got to Oxford yet."

"We never shall if I get caught by the dawn."

"What an odd thing to say."

"You're pretty dense for an intelligent man."

"Forget it. The catkins were out, the sun was warm. I became as I always do in the spring, light of heart in spite of the war."

"Which hadn't really begun."

"Which hadn't really begun. But the blackbirds had. There were snowdrops out in the garden. I bought my usual pots of azaleas and hydrangeas."

"You haven't mentioned flowers before."

"That's not because I don't love them. I love the smell of hyacinths, the sight of tulips and daffodils and anemones and crocuses. The larks began carolling above the Downs. I was elected President of the local Dramatic Club. Jill and I walked over the Downs and hunted on foot in the Weald. I must have been making a bit of money because I put £100 into War Loan. I began broadcasting about poetry to the B.E.F. I sold my spy story, *The Man in Blue Glasses*, to Hutchinson. Lalage got measles, and my father, who came down from Derbyshire to stay with us, suddenly cracked up and went home again. There was a bad day in April when Jill was set upon by a madman on the Downs who frightened her so much that she daren't go out anywhere alone.

"When I made out my income-tax return I found that I had made over £600 broadcasting and £400 advertising. Altogether in spite of the war I had made about £1,200. I did some more broadcasting from Bristol, Manchester and London and heard one of my talks played back. While I'm giving the talks they seem they're all right. Played back they seem all wrong, too fast, too indistinct, plain dull. I get depressed when I fail to come up to standard."

"Whose standard?"

"Mine, of course," I said irritably. "Why laugh?"

"It suddenly occurred to me what a poisonous time Jill must have with you."

"What on earth?"

"Do you remember Fergus Crampton?"

"Who's he?"

"In *You Never Can Tell.*"

"Of course I remember him."

"Then why ask who he was?"

"I wasn't thinking."

"You often don't."

"What about Crampton?"

"Do you remember Shaw's stage direction about him?"

"N-no. I've forgotten."

" 'An atrociously obstinate, ill-tempered, grasping mouth and a dogmatic voice.' He must have been thinking of you. That's why they stopped you broadcasting. Your standard's too high. You've never learnt to take it easy."

"I do my best."

Again she laughed.

"If only now and again you wouldn't. Anyway, don't mind me. Go on."

It was my turn to laugh. I was turning over the pages of my diary for 1940. I came across a reply that I had written to an editor who had accused me of "wearing thin". I handed it to Penelope.

"You'd better read this."

She read it and handed it back.

"Dr. Johnson had nothing on you when it comes to invective. No wonder you never held a job down. Are you always so rude?"

"Almost invariably."

"I wonder you're alive. Men have been shot for much less than this. You can abuse yourself, but when anybody else abuses you you call down fire from Heaven."

"I don't. I create my fire myself."

I began to turn over the pages hurriedly. Is it true that I can't take adverse criticism?

"On 6th May I was broadcasting in Manchester and was driven back to my Derbyshire home by my father, who was then eighty-one years and four days old. It was sheer hell. I sweated with terror. He hadn't any idea how to drive and cursed my head off when I asked him to go more slowly."

I turned over some more pages.

Then came the day that Germany invaded Holland, Belgium and Luxemburg, and began bombing French and English towns. The war had at last begun. I still have a card asking me to attend a meeting of the L.D.V.

"I decided that for Lalage's and Imogen's sake we ought to leave Sussex and go up to my father in Derbyshire. 'If we leave here,' said Jill, 'we'll never come back.' On the 29th May we sent Lalage, Imogen and Nanny up to Tansley. We followed the next day. That was the day of the evacuation from Dunkirk."

You know the way a room suddenly goes all still and quiet and empty?

I turned round.

Penelope wasn't there.

As I looked at the settee I heard a cock crow. I looked out of the window. It was still dark, but I could see in the east the first faint streaks of dawn. I shivered.

What was this? I whispered to myself, "The Lord be with you." Like the wind whispering in the trees came the reply:

"And with Blithe Spirit."

"That's what I thought you said," I whispered.

I settled down to my work. So well did I settle that the next thing I heard was Jill's voice.

"That's funny. Don't tell me that you've been to my drawer."

"I've never been near your drawer."

"Then perhaps you can explain this scent?"

I got up and went over to the settee.

"You're right," I said. "That's the scent you used when I first knew you."

"Thanks for the memory. How did it get here? Have you been entertaining a wench?"

"Just an angel unawares," I said. "A blithe spirit. Your blithe spirit."

# CHAPTER V

## LAST DAYS AT TANSLEY RECTORY (1940)

I WAS just about to start to tell you of my last days at Tansley, the village where my father was Rector for fifty-two years and I was brought up, when I heard a faint rustle, turned round and saw my divine Zenocrate—I mean Penelope—sitting on the settee knitting, or rather unravelling. The time was just 3.15 a.m.

My heart leapt up.

"The Lord be with you," I said gravely.

"And with Blithe Spirit," she replied less gravely.

"What?"

She repeated it.

"That's what I thought you said," I said.

"That's what I did say," she replied demurely.

"Where were we?"

"Dunkirk."

"Funny your remembering that."

"I remember that you had left Toad Hall and gone back to your father's rectory at Tansley. Go on from there."

"Well," I said, "as I was a member of the L.D.V. in Sussex I naturally made it my business to become a member of the L.D.V. in Derbyshire. Instead of guarding the South Downs I had to defend the limestone crags of the Peak. I well remember my first night. There were two rifles in the hut, one marked 'Loaded', the other marked 'Not loaded'. I tried the one marked 'Not loaded'. They'd got it wrong.

"Tansley was my father's first and only living. We went there in 1890 when I was five years old. Both my parents were Devonians, used to warmth and sunshine and a soft-spoken, slow but kindly people. The transition was abrupt. My mother never took to the change. She always regarded herself as an alien, which indeed she was. It must have been hell for her."

"Why didn't they get out?"

"Because nobody wants to live in a Derbyshire mining and quarry village if he can help it. They used to advertise for an exchange every week of the year in *The Church Times*. Sometimes they exchanged for a year, never more. I was too young to know what I was missing. They used to send me back for long periods to my aunts on the farm at Yarde. They neither of them liked children, but I was happy anywhere, happy damming up the tiny streams in front of the farm at Yarde, equally happy at Tansley exploring wilder waters to their source high up on the grouse moors. I was always completely happy in my own society. I never felt lonely. I have never felt lonely. People are always coming out with silly cracks about the bad luck of being an only child. I loved being an only child. I should have hated any brothers and sisters. Jill says that they would have smoothed my edges. I prefer my edges rough. I owe that to Derbyshire. It is a rough country. The records of the Sherwood Foresters prove that. If I wanted to climb Mount Everest I'd take a nucleus of Tansley men, who were boys when I was a boy, who were at the National School with me. They're a proud, independent community. My mother always insisted that they were descended from the convicts (as she called them) whom the Romans used as forced labour in the lead-mines. They may well have been. I don't mind convicts. I had a good opportunity of studying them at close quarters when my father exchanged jobs temporarily with the Chaplain at Portland. He was the only man we could find willing to live in Tansley for a change.

"The main trouble with Tansley was that the sun never shone. A thick grey pall of fog and smoke—most depressing—hung over the valley of Matlock below and the Castle of Riber on the hill above. I don't know when I became a sun-worshipper, probably when I went to live in Sussex where the sun always shines. All I know is that it is my life-blood. I get so ill in Oxford that I'm continually feeling like death. I live in a state of deadly inertia here. As soon as I get to Switzerland I come to life again. It's odd. It's the same with hills. I'm miserable away from hills. Oxford has no hills. I once refused a job in Lewes—the Directorship of Education—because of its lack of hills. I didn't count Mount Caburn on the South Downs as a hill, though Gilbert White called those little bumps majestical mountains. I owe to Derbyshire my capacity to endure long distances. I ran up and down those hills. I ran for Derby County and I ran for Oxford. I found that easy, though not particularly pleasant. Track-running is tedious, as tedious as rowing (my father's pursuit). Give me Rugger, cricket, tennis, any team game, and of course ski-ing. I played for Tansley at every game they played, not well, but roughly. In point of fact we had to be tough. I remember a game against Youlgreave, a remote village up one of the

smaller dales, when we were stoned out of the village because we had
dared to win. That was football. It was at Youlgreave that I wit-
nessed a scene which lent colour to my mother's theory about the
Roman convicts. It was a Saturday evening. I've forgotten the name
of the pub. What I do remember is a man kneeling on the table with
his hands tied behind his back fighting with his teeth a live rat that
was suspended from the hanging paraffin lamp in the middle of the
room. *Nil alienum*, etc. That's me. But for once I was revolted. I felt
quite sick at the sight of this strange combat.

"There was the bookie at Clay Cross who came into the changing
tent and offered me a £5 note if I would pull the race, that is, run
second instead of first in the mile. It caused a really rough house
when he found that I wouldn't play.

"Going back home to the scene of one's childhood is always
exciting. I missed my mother, who had died the year before. I missed
her much more than my father did. He was now his own master, a
free man to come and go as he liked, and on the whole I think he
liked his freedom, though he struck me as unduly frail for so strong
a man. You have to remember that he had always worked with his
hands. He took in the coal, dug up the garden, whitewashed the
outside walls of the house, tinkered about with the car, sawed wood,
lopped the trees, and mended the garden wall. He was one of the
best all-rounders I have ever met and I admired enormously his
skill with his hands. I remember when the Ecclesiastical Commissioners decided that the fungus that was eating its way through the
dining-room floor must be destroyed he refused to employ anyone
to do it. He took up the floor-boards himself, and he made an
extremely good job of it. It tired him out and made him irritable,
which was foreign to his nature. It was his nature to be silent.

" 'Brodie,' my mother would say after a long harangue in the
drawing-room, 'have you gone stone deaf?'

"He had a wonderful capacity for not listening to anything that
was said to him.

"Normally in the evenings my mother would sit at her little
desk writing, as I thought, letters to her sisters. In point of fact she
was studying finance. We didn't discover this until after her death.
We had always lived from hand to mouth, always scraped and
screwed and watched every penny. We formed a club and after
binding the *Quiver*, *Sunday at Home*, *Strand*, *Cornhill* and *Temple
Bar* in brown paper covers, subscribers sent their particular choice
round the club each Monday. So we saw all the magazines and

only paid for one. All three of us were omnivorous readers. My father had a passion for the classics, my mother for the ultra-moderns. I read anything and everything. The consequence was that after washing up at nights we settled down in silence, each with a book, in front of the fire. We were seldom disturbed by callers. There were no gentry in the village, and my mother was a stickler for the conventions of the day. She would have nothing to do with the neighbouring clergy, but she cultivated the local doctor and bank manager. I was occasionally drawn in to play cards but normally I refused to join their coterie. The bank manager's daughters were not my cup of tea at all in spite of the fact that they were 'County'. My taste was low. I used to make my friends among the mill-hands, and the quarrymen's and nursery-gardeners' daughters, and I would spend long dark winter evenings sitting on a stone stile or in a wet dripping cave with Gertie, Carrie or Ivy. We didn't talk much. We never worried about the wind and the rain. The more my mother abused me for the company I kept the more I liked it.

"We were a rather gay village. We were always getting up socials and dances. I sang, I recited, I danced, I played round games like 'Postman's Knock', 'Forfeits', and 'Spin the Trencher'.

"It was strange to be back at the age of fifty-five with a war on and all my old friends looking very old indeed.

"I went round the cottages to visit as many as were still alive. They were all cordial in their welcome, as North country people invariably are, but there was a great gulf fixed between us. I had got out and they had stayed put. I was moving in a different society. On my first day the Duchess of Devonshire asked me if I could do anything to stimulate the recruiting of the Women's Land Army.

"After joining the local L.D.V. I spent a lot of time shooting on the range to keep my hand in. I was detailed to guard a post on Beely Moor, which stands about 1,100 feet above sea level. My hours of duty were 6.30 p.m. to twelve midnight on Tuesdays and Fridays. I had forgotten how lovely and wild this country is. We stalked foxes and caught a young owl, listened to the curlew and watched the plover. After the Sussex coast it was all extraordinarily peaceful.

"The disadvantage about being marooned in Derbyshire was the difficulty of travelling to and from London and Bristol, where I was broadcasting most days. In addition to my broadcasts I was kept busy travelling round the country, lecturing to Women's Institutes on war-time cooking, about which I knew nothing beyond what the Ministry of Food told me. I was lucky in having had the invaluable experience that I had gained during the years of depression when I had visited the worst areas—Merseyside, Tyneside, South Wales, Cumberland, Durham and the rest, inciting the unemployed to make the most they could out of the little they'd got. This was an exact parallel. Food was again short and everyone wanted to know how to make the very little go the longest possible way.

"My talks on the air had been far more successful than I had ever dared to hope, mainly because I was determined to turn the business of cooking into an entertainment. We had lots of fun. There was the day when Lionel Gamlin introduced me on the air as 'Your old runner bean' and the day when Bruce Belfrage, after a particularly gay bit of nonsense, played me out by saying, 'And that, believe it or not, ladies and gentlemen, was your old friend S. P. B. Mais.'

"I think that was the day that the Ministry wanted me to plug rose-hip juice. And I did it by saying: 'Don't tell me that rose hasn't any hips. I know better.' One listener turned the phrase to music and I sang a lyric in praise of rose's hips to an astonished world. The high-ups in the Ministry of Food disapproved of my method. But they couldn't deny that I had achieved the aim they had in mind, to popularize rose-hips.

" 'It's men like you make women like me like men like you,' was typical of the sort of letter that came in after my rose-hip talk.

"Some fans burst into verse:

> "I think that we shall never see
> The face of Mr. 'S. P. B.'
> But oh! his voice we like to hear,
> It fills the day with such good cheer.
> So will the kindly B.B.C.
> Still spare some time to 'S. P. B.'!

"I was getting people out of bed earlier in the morning.

> "Inclined in the morning to LAIS,
> (My mind in a bit of a DAIS),
> I'll admit I may Muse,
> Through the 8 o'clock NUSE,
> But I REVEILLE in S. P. B. MAIS.

" 'Carry on, Silas Ponsonby Bartholomew,' wrote somebody from Harpenden; 'continue to "A MAIS" and cheer us—we like it.' "

"Several, of course, didn't.

" 'Not so much of the ladies, more recipes, please.' "

Penelope laughed.

"Yes, I imagine that's always been your Achilles' heel."

"And why not?" I said. "I work infinitely better as the result of your being here. You're a real tonic to me."

"You were talking about food," she said.

I took the hint.

" 'The Kitchen Front' was a crusade. It was grand to feel that I really was being of some use after all, but it struck me after a time that the series would be improved if I didn't always occupy the platform myself, so I gradually turned it over to a committee of experts. I didn't want to abandon the child that I had created, but for the sake of the cause it seemed to me to be wise. In many ways this was my finest hour. I've certainly done nothing since that has made me feel so pleased with myself."

Penelope's gaze strayed to the mantelpiece which contains four photographs in frames, three of Imogen and one of Lalage. Above it is their portrait, painted when Lalage was twelve and Imogen was seven by the Radley Art Master at a cost of thirty guineas.

"I should have thought that bringing up those two was equally worth while."

"To me personally, yes. It's been a strain keeping them both at Cheltenham. When we were at Tansley I sent Lalage to a convent in Matlock and Imogen stayed at home. The war came hard on children. Lalage was first at a national school in Devon, then at a small school in Shoreham, then at this convent in Matlock, and later at the Dragon School, Oxford. She never had a chance to have a continuously reasonable education."

"She's lovely to look at, and charming."

"Lovely to look at, and charming. I agree."

"How did they react to Tansley?"

"It was a hot summer. They missed the sea. My father was eighty-one and became peevish with Imogen, who was everybody's darling but his. He reduced her to tears by his harshness, which was odd for him, because he wasn't by nature harsh."

"Just getting old."

"Just getting old. You can't expect octogenarians to see eye to eye with three-year-olds. They had one thing in common."

"What was that?"

"A love of water. Putts (as we called my father), Jill, Lalage, Imogen and I all bathed in the Lido at Matlock. That was fun. Lalage used to go for long walks with me over the moors. She was a darling child. She was eight then.

"I was away a good deal, giving these 'Kitchen Front' talks in London. I remember on 17th June that I had to go on the air immediately after France had fallen. We had luncheon with Philip Noel Baker that day. He was in the depths of gloom. We had our first air-raid on 19th June while we were spending the night in Brighton with my doctor. We sat up all night discussing Yeats' poetry."

"You didn't mind the raids?"

"I loathed them. They always gave me a sinking feeling in the pit of my stomach. I wasn't so frightened as I had been in the First World War.

"When I went back to Derbyshire I was in great request in all the villages at the Women's Institutes, where I followed up my 'Kitchen Front' talks with demonstrations. The air-raids then descended on Derbyshire. There were bomb craters all over the village. I took Jill and the children up to Southport, where I gave more 'Kitchen Front' demonstrations. From there I went to Manchester, where I had several very lively meetings, some from a food-van at the street corners. I had another mobile unit at Liverpool. I was back in Southport to celebrate my fifty-fifth birthday and noted the fact in my diary that 'Nothing in life is so sweet and moving as the sight of Lalage and Imogen asleep in bed with their toys ranged on their pillows and they scarcely breathing.' Their toys have always meant a lot to them. Lalage at twenty still takes her dolls to bed with her. I don't know what that's a sign of. Imogen carries her dolls all over the world.

"It's odd, this curious catch in the throat that I get whenever I see Imogen asleep. At fifteen she still sings her two little hymns to Jill and myself before she goes to sleep. 'Jesus bits of shine' instead of 'Jesus bids us shine', and a hymn of her own invention, 'Good night little rabbits all over the world'. Both these songs almost move me to tears.

"Lalage even then, at the age of nine, showed a tendency to be the cat that walks by itself.

"I found myself resenting the stopping of church bells. It was as fatuous as the uprooting of all road sign-posts. The Germans knew their way about England better than any Englishman. Their maps were far more detailed and accurate and up to date than ours.

"From Liverpool I went back to London to give more 'Kitchen Front' talks. I got tremendous help from Lord Woolton, who was one of the most genial and accessible men I ever worked under. Almost alone among my chiefs he praised my talks. I even got him to give up time to come to a Foyle's Luncheon, where I made my usual irresponsible and uncorrelated speech and he his usual suave, happily phrased one. How is it that those Conservative Cabinet Ministers, always overworked, can get up in public and speak as if they had nothing to do in life but give speeches? This isn't true of all politicians. I listened last night to a Labour M.P. talking in 'The Week in Westminster' and he seemed to go out of his way to drop as many h's as he could. I regard dropped h's in speech as much an indication of mental laziness as dropped catches in the cricket field are signs of physical laziness, and I regard with a good deal of mistrust a government where no care is taken to speak the King's English. It shows a disrespect to His Majesty and a contempt for conventional usage.

"To go back for a minute to Lord Woolton. When I first asked him to come to the luncheon he refused because:

(a) He expected London to be invaded before the day of the luncheon.

(b) He thought it bad policy to be seen in an expensive restaurant.

(c) He thought he would be accused of wasting his time.

It says volumes for his character that he took the trouble to tell me why he couldn't come, and then had the courage to change his mind. I seemed to be about as hard-worked as ever I have been in my life. One day I was on the air giving a 'Kitchen Front' talk in London, the next in Manchester, the next talking to a girls' school evacuated to Chatsworth, the next preaching two sermons in Tansley Church. The date of those sermons was 14th July, 1940. We celebrated two great occasions in one day, the centenary of the building of the church, and my father's jubilee as Rector. Fifty years in the same parish means something. I always admired my father but never so much as on that day. With characteristic modesty he summed up his fifty years' devotion to this intractable village by giving a bare catalogue of the christenings, marriages and burials that he had taken.

" 'We have paid our way,' he said, and then as a testimonial to himself accepted a new boiler for the church.

" 'In 1890,' he said, 'I was sent here as a sick young priest about to die. I am not, thanks to you, quite so delicate in 1940 as I was in 1890.'

"I can still see the twinkle in his eye as he said that. I wish I had his sense of humour, his poise, and his certainty about this life and the next. He lived so much within himself that I never knew him. Whether at any time in his long life he ever wanted to know me I never knew. I never took him into my confidence. As a small boy I used to like going round with him delivering the parish magazines. They were silent rides. He never said a word and yet I enjoyed them enormously. It is quite likely that he yearned to know his son, but I am not the sort of person to yearn over satisfactorily.

"I took great pains over the preparation of my Tansley memories. I reminded the village of its good fortune in being built on a rock of gritstone which gave them hills and dales of unsurpassed beauty, and bred in them hardihood, steadfastness and individuality.

"I reminded them of local worthies: Florence Nightingale, Anthony Babington and Phoebe Bowen, who walked forty miles a day, drove a team of horses, thatched barns, broke in intractable foals, could make her voice carry a mile, read Milton, Pope and Shakespeare, and played the bass viol in church.

"I then talked to the greybeards and baldheads, men who had been boys when I was a boy and had honoured me through life by calling me by my Christian name.

"I called the roll of them. Some of them weren't there. They had been killed in the First World War.

"This was the first time in my life that I had addressed my own people. I was terribly nervous. I had been to the ends of the earth, and become, most unexpectedly, one of the most famous men in England. Quickly I ran over in review the good times that we had shared in youth, bathing in the mill-dam, dancing at the village socials, flirting with the girls, walking over the hills.

"The rolling stone had returned. The only thing to be said in my favour was that I had gathered no moss.

"There were things that I should have learnt had I stayed put. I should have learnt thrift. Country folk don't regard borrowers with a glad eye. I felt that I had wasted my life. And yet—and yet—I am by nature restless. Tansley wasn't really big enough for me.

"I cannot rest from travel: I will drink
Life to the lees: all times I have enjoy'd
Greatly, have suffer'd greatly, both with those
That loved me, and alone . . .
                    I am become a name:
For always roaming with a hungry heart
Much have I seen and known . . .
How dull it is to pause, to make an end,
To rust unburnish'd, not to shine in use,
As tho' to breathe were life.

"There's really not much point in repining about life. If I had
my time over again what should I have done? Exactly what I have
done. I needn't have been so extravagant, I needn't have made so
many mistakes. I needn't have had the luxuries I have enjoyed, but
I've had a magnificent life. I'm not complaining.

"I'm not blind or a cripple. I'm in possession of such faculties
as I have. I've got the sun in the morning and the moon at night,
so I'm all right. When I pray to God I thank Him, and I've got a
lot to thank Him for. I've had a happy life.

"I went back to London the day after the centenary and
jubilee celebrations and had a row with the Ministry of Food about
milk.

"I was offered a fantastic sum to go on the music-halls. That
shows how popular a figure I had become. It was during that week
that I had my first lunch with Norman Birkett, who later suggested
that I should write *Buffets and Rewards*. I was getting between 400
and 500 letters a day from admirers of the 'Kitchen Front' talks.

"I gave the last of them on 20th July, 1940. I was then free to go
back to Lalage and Imogen and have a rest, and did I need it?

"I ran into a lot of bombing, but that was part of the ordinary
routine of those days. Lalage used to get terribly frightened. I
walked with her to the top of Masson, our nearest hill. I went out
pigeon-shooting with the local rat-catcher."

"Forgive my interrupting you," said Penelope. "But a thought
has just occurred to me."

"Sorry," I said. "I was carried away. I've been talking too much
as usual."

"It's not that. I've been wondering what you think about your
Autobiography."

"Trollope's," I said, "was better."

"I can't remember Trollope's."

"Well, as a change from mine, let me read you the last page or two of his. You'll see the difference."

I went over to my bookshelf and pulled out the well-thumbed Trollope.

"It's the best thing he wrote. Listen."

I began:

" 'It will not, I am sure, be thought that, in making my boast as to quantity, I have endeavoured to lay claim to any literary excellence.' That's me, exactly. 150 books! Not much quality. 'That, in the writing of books, quantity without quality is a vice and a misfortune, has been too manifestly settled to leave a doubt on such a matter. But I do lay claim to whatever merit should be accorded to me for persevering diligence in my profession.' Yes, I think I can make that claim too. 'And I make the claim, not with a view to my own glory, but for the benefit of those who may read these pages when young and who may intend to follow the same career. *Nulla dies sine linea*. Let that be their motto. And let their work be to them as is his common work to the common lecturer. No gigantic efforts will then be necessary. He need tie no wet towels round his brow, nor sit for thirty hours at his desk without moving—as men have sat, or said that they have sat. More than nine-tenths of my literary work has been done in the last twenty years and during twelve of those years I followed also another profession.' That's true of me, too. 'I have never been a slave to this work, giving due time, if not more than due time, to the amusements I have loved.' Hunting in his case, hunting in mine, riding, cricket, ski-ing, the theatre, travelling all over the place. Meeting people. No, like Trollope, I've never been a slave to my work. Jill wouldn't let me be, anyway."

"Go on with Trollope."

"Right. 'But I have been constant. And constancy in labour will conquer all difficulties . . . It may interest some if I state that during the last twenty years I have made by literature something near £70,000.' £70,000! What couldn't I have done with £70,000?"

" 'I look upon the result as comfortable, but not splendid.' I'll say it's comfortable. Look at this cesspool of a study."

"It suits you."

"Does it? 'It will not, I trust, be supposed by any reader that I have intended in this so-called autobiography to give a record of my inner life. No man ever did so truly—and no man ever will.' Won't they? I've done it. Of course you've got to record your inner life. It's dishonest not to. One's inner life is really the whole of one's life."

LALAGE, IMOGEN AND JILL IN IRELAND

PETRE, LALAGE AND IMOGEN HUNTING IN WALES

IMOGEN, LALAGE AND JILL IN LLANWRTYD

IMOGEN IN NORWAY

JILL IN IRELAND

PETRE IN IRELAND

THE FAMILY AT SHREWSBURY

"Go on."

" 'Rousseau probably attempted it, but who doubts but that Rousseau has confessed in much the thoughts and convictions rather than the facts of life?' And what's wrong with thoughts and convictions? I suppose Trollope had no thoughts and no convictions. 'If the rustle of a woman's petticoat has ever stirred my blood. If I have thought tobacco at midnight in pleasant company to be one of the elements of an earthly Paradise . . .' I'd put snuff first, tobacco second. I like both. 'If now and again I have somewhat recklessly fluttered a £5 note over a card-table.' Not guilty. I hate cards, except Canasta and Rummy with Imogen. 'Of what interest is that to any reader? I have betrayed no woman. Wine has brought me no sorrow.' That's true. 'It has been the companionship of smoking that I have loved, rather than the habit.' True again. 'I have never desired to còin money, and I have lost none.' I have always desired to coin money, and I haven't lost a terrible lot. 'To enjoy the excitement of pleasure, but to be free from its vices and ill-effects—to have the sweets and leave the bitter untasted—that has been my study.' I'm not so methodical. I've taken the bitter with the sweet. I'm not complaining. 'The preachers tell us this is impossible. It seems to me that hitherto I have succeeded fairly well. I will not say that I have never scorched a finger, but I carry no ugly wounds.' "

"Well!"

"Do I carry any ugly wounds? I don't think so."

"Water off a duck's back."

"Maybe."

" 'For what remains to me of life I trust for my happiness chiefly to my work'—Yes, so do I—'hoping that when the power of work be over with me, God may be pleased to take me from a world in which, according to my creed, there can then be no joy.' How true. How true. 'Secondly, to the love of those who love me.' I couldn't agree more. 'And then to my books . . . That I can read, and be happy while I am reading, is a great blessing.' I'll say it is. 'Could I have remembered, as some men do, what I read, I should have been able to call myself an educated man.' How like I am to Trollope.

"On 18th August I went back to London to give more 'Kitchen Front' talks. There were raids every night. I remember that one of my talks was on tinned food. I told the world that no tinned food ever went bad and that you could keep it pretty well for

F

ever with impunity. We had bought about a hundred tins of food about a year before and I dared not eat it in spite of what I said. My mother's influence was still strong on me even after her death. I'm terrified of ptomaine poisoning. By day I went down to Osterley to attend a Home Guard course.

"When we went back to Tansley we were raided every night, so it didn't matter whether we stayed in London or the country. We spent our days exploring the loveliness of Dovedale and the other little dales for a book that I was writing on the countryside.

"We bought a new bedroom suite for fifty guineas. In point of fact it turned out to be a bargain. In any event I had plenty of money, enough anyway to lend my father £100.

"We went up to Fortingall in September, taking Lalage but not Imogen with us. We did some grand walks round Schiehallion and Ben Lawers, and up Glen Lyon. Lalage proved a grand little walker.

"I showed her stags and eagles. On our return at the end of the month I entered her at the convent in Matlock, and Jill and I then went up to Ilkley to stay with my cousins. We fished the Ribble. We visited Sterne's house at Coxwold. I wrote lots of articles and another spy novel.

"Then in November came the blitz of Coventry and all the Hun aeroplanes made their rendezvous over Tansley, making a hell of a noise. From then on we had them over every night and the 'Alerts' used to be on for ten hours at a time. I learnt to plough in order to talk to schools on country pursuits.

"Then one day at the beginning of December my father threw Lalage's clothes out of the dining-room and Imogen out of the kitchen, so I decided that we'd better go back to Shoreham.

"On 9th January, 1941, my Brighton doctor drove up to Derbyshire in order to take us back home for the last time. I said goodbye to my childhood home without regrets. I had outstayed my welcome. My father was ageing rapidly and resented the presence of children.

"You remember those lines of W. B. Yeats:

"Our souls
Are love, and a continual farewell."

There was no answer.

"Surely," I said, "you must remember that? It's one of the most moving things ever said by . . ."

I turned round.

There was no one there, just the dent in the settee, and the scent that Jill used when I first met her.

"Well, well," I said, "the Lord be with you."

"And with Blithe Spirit," came a whisper from I don't know where.

# CHAPTER VI

## I Come Back to Oxford (1941)

"How long have you had this house?" asked Penelope.

I looked round the overcrowded untidy study.

"Doesn't it look like me?" I said.

"It's you all right. I was just wondering how long it took you to leave your mark and make things and people yours."

"People no time at all, houses a bit longer. When we first came here, in 1941, bombed out of home, I promised Jill that we should be back in six weeks. We've been here ten years. I shall die here."

"From choice?"

"From choice. It's semi-detached, a thing I loathe, it's in a town, and I hate towns. It's in the most unhealthy town I ever lived in, but it's become me. My roots are in. I'm not going in spite of the paddock."

"The paddock?"

I pointed out of the window.

"What's wrong with the paddock?"

"Now? Nothing. It's my continual inspiration. I have the squirrels in the morning and the owl at night. I'm all right. But the trees are coming down, the green open space is to disappear. Buildings are going up. They're going to put up a school—an Elementary School."

"You don't think much of Elementary Schools?"

"I was at one."

"Yes. I remember you told me, at Tansley."

"Well: we went back to Toad Hall—but not for long."

"A continual farewell?"

"Precisely. At first we were only too glad to be back, free to do as we liked in our own home, yet not so free. There was the black-out. There was the never-to-be-forgotten day when Jill and I were turned off our own Downs. We came across a ewe lambing and ran down the gully to fetch the shepherd. On our way we were accosted by a whipper-snapper of a subaltern who questioned our right to be on the Downs at all. Jill burst into tears. I cursed his head off and he wanted to put me under arrest as a spy. I insisted on fetching the shepherd and made him come with me, but the Downs were lost to us thereafter, Nature at one entrance quite shut out. We were close to the harbour. That was closed to us. The beach was mined. There was an airfield within a few hundred yards and the Germans bombed it regularly every breakfast-time, every lunch-time, and every dinner-time. Then they took to machine-gunning Lalage and Imogen as they took their morning walk. I realize now that we ought never to have gone back, but it was home, and Jill said that she would rather die there than live anywhere else. We stuck it out for quite a time, until 27th March, to be accurate.

"Jill and I were away most of the time as I was broadcasting from Bristol, where we also got our fair share of bombs. Every time I waved good-bye to Lalage and Imogen I thought it was for the last time.

"How we got out of Bristol alive I don't know. The whole of George Street went up in flames one night, and the next morning there was nothing but cats sitting among the smoking ruins and telephone bells ringing. We stayed sometimes at St. Vincent's Rocks Hotel and sometimes at Chipping Sodbury, where we got a dress-circle view of the bombing of Bristol and of Cardiff, and on the night Bath went up we had evacuees from that city to look after.

"There were times when I found broadcasting quite a pain in the neck. You see, I'm terrified of noise. If bombs were silent, like lightning, I shouldn't mind them half so much, but I jump about a foot in the air whenever a motor-car tyre bursts. On the stage, if a pistol is going to be fired, I plug my ears and miss all the dialogue. I've inherited that from my mother, who was terrified of thunder but not of lightning. I've always felt it a bit unfair that war should be such a noisy affair. I don't think that I'm really a coward. I could fight bravely enough in a war fought with knives. I was born in the wrong age. I'm reduced to a pulp by the noise of big guns. The curious thing is that I was now broadcasting about hedging and ditching to schools and recommending books like *Martin Chuzzlewit*. It didn't seem to be helping to win the war.

"I remember being a good deal perturbed on 15th January because a man in a quite high position whom I had been seeing quite a lot murdered his wife because he couldn't let her endure the poverty that he saw coming.

"Added to that I had Nanny in bed as well as Imogen. My only comfort came from the cawing of the rooks in the copse outside Toad Hall. That, and the stars at night. It's odd how I've always been consoled by looking up at the stars at night. I'm not any good at guessing what they are, Betelgeuse and all that lot. I know the North Star, Orion's Belt and the Plough, and that's about all.

"The stars put life and death into proper perspective. A fat lot Venus and Jupiter and Saturn care whether Bristol or Shoreham is bombed. I stand under the stars and just gaze in wonder and say 'Wonderbar!' or something equally ineffective.

"It was in this same week that Archie Macdonell, who wrote that lovely book *England, Their England*, died an untimely death at Oxford.

"I was working hard on disc drills and things to do with farming for my broadcasts by day and fire-watching by night. The church at Southwick went up in flames. Hutchinsons rang up to tell me that my spy story *The Black Spider* had been destroyed in the raid of 29th December, together with all my other books, so Jill had to sit down and retype the whole story. I went up to talk to a girls' school at Abbot's Bromley. I seemed to be spending my days in terrible train journeys. No heat, no food, overcrowded and unpunctual. Yet I was always on time for my broadcasts.

"There's an entry in my diary for 9th February, 1941, which runs: 'What shall we remember as we look back on all this? The long anxiety of the tension? Each house with "stirrup-pump" in red letters in the window, the ladders up to the roofs, the sand-bags and buckets ready, the cards with the number of occupants of the house written up on the gate-post and the windows in case they had to dig our bodies out.' That was ghoulish, if you like.

"Or should we remember the scarcity of marmalade, onions, sugar, tea, oranges, bananas, meat and cheese?

"Imogen never saw a banana till after the war, but she made me get off a bus in Brighton once because she saw coloured cardboard bananas hanging in a shop-window.

"What do I remember of all that? Absolutely nothing until I refer to my diary. That shows you how easy it is to forget terrors. That explains why prisoners of war even in Japanese camps bear so little trace of the hell that they went through.

"Among the things that struck me as noteworthy were paying 16s. 7d. for a chicken and the fact that we still could follow the Crawley and Horsham on foot. On St. Valentine's Day the children were inoculated against diphtheria and I got my first war-time news of Priscilla who had been taken by the Germans at Amiens in May, 1940. She was in Paris on 30th October.

"A publisher offered me £50 for the copyright of my 'Kitchen Front' talks, which I accepted.

"Jill finished retyping *The Black Spider*, and I took it to be bound during an air-raid.

"Christopher Stone then invited me to join him in his 'Anniversaries' programme, which took a good deal of research but helped to keep us out of the workhouse. I remember being called on by a boy called Nicholson, an airman, who had been awarded the V.C. He was an Old Tonbridge boy and I gave him my very valuable Tattershall Dodd print of Tonbridge. It was the least I could do.

"On the 8th March Shoreham became a Prohibited Area. We debated where to go this time and decided that Oxford was the best bid.

"A friend of mine who had been up at Oxford with me was still living in a village just outside and he offered us hospitality while we were looking round.

"I was delighted. 'If we go,' said Jill, 'we shall never come back.' 'Nonsense,' I said. 'I swear we'll be back within six months.'

"We went up to see Christopherson and fixed to go in about a fortnight. We sent the children on in advance on 21st March, and on the 27th, a day when Shoreham had five raids, we followed.

"Christopherson's house was old, a place of stone floors, oak panels, low beams and all that. It was a good hide-out for the children while Jill and I were broadcasting from London and Bristol. We didn't feel that they were likely to be bombed while we were away.

"I found the Oxford climate enervating and almost unbearable after Sussex. There was no sun and no air. I felt sleepy all the time.

"I worked in the Bodleian on my 'Anniversaries' programme.

"One day I sat next to a white-haired man whose breath stank and whose socks were mainly holes. He told me that he had been in my form at Rossall and was engaged on a thesis to prove that Christ wasn't crucified on Good Friday. He also told me that he had taken a First in 'Greats'.

"On 1st May Lalage went to the Dragon School. The next day was my father's eighty-second birthday.

"On 27th May I was broadcasting in Bristol when the news came through that we had sunk the *Bismarck*. The man in the tram by my side waved his arms at the ruined city and said, 'That pays for all that.' Could, I thought, evil ever pay for evil? An eye destroyed doesn't necessarily make the other blind man see.

"On 20th June I was summoned to Tansley as my father was

dying. Four days later we left Christopherson and took up our quarters at 91 St. Aldate's, Oxford, a lovely house just opposite Christ Church. On 27th June we went up to Tansley again to see my father, who had taken a turn for the better. On 8th July we went up again and found my father in hospital, very angry with the rat-catcher for using his car without asking leave. On 27th July my father died and we saw him in the mortuary looking like a mediaeval abbot carved in stone. I had an interview with the solicitors, who told me that he had left nothing. An odd thing was that Naylor, the parson at Ashover, died on the same day, aged eighty-three, having held his living for fifty-three years. So my father beat him in the race to Heaven by a short head.

"The funeral took place in drenching rain.

" 'Lovely and pleasant in their lives, in their deaths they were not divided' was the text I had carved on the granite tombstone that I put above the grave of my father and mother. The Ecclesiastical Commissioners at first refused to grant me leave to use the text as they contended that it was not in the Bible.

"I gave my father's watch to Imogen and she said, 'I'll give it back to him in Heaven.'

"The thing I couldn't get used to was the fact that I should no longer hear from him or be able to write to him. We had always been good correspondents. He always wrote to me on the backs of envelopes.

"In September we went up to Fortingall and spent a glorious fortnight climbing over the Grampians before returning to Tansley to sort out the furniture and decide what to sell. On 21st September we left the Rectory for the last time. A week later we moved into this house, which was then furnished. We had to pay six guineas a week. I approved of the paddock which faces the study and I approved of the view over the river to Wytham Woods at the back of the house. Jill was very much surprised at the failure of laundry, bread, milk, beer and so on to arrive. Oxford we discovered was the home of unfulfilled promises as well as of lost causes. I was in London most days doing the 'Anniversaries' programme. The boiler burst, the radio set refused to function, and everything failed to work. I began to teach at the Dragon. The climate of Oxford quickly got me down. I was earning practically nothing and paying out far more than I got in.

"Imogen and Lalage both ran high temperatures and had to stay in bed, and both Jill and I got so depressed that on the 25th

November we decided to go back to Shoreham. As soon as we decided to go home I became undecided. We had no home and no friends and felt utterly deserted.

"Suddenly I was invited to write the history of a paper-mill for 300 guineas. On 16th December we went back to have a last look at Toad Hall. So ended 1941.

"On 6th February, 1942, I started to teach at Radley."

"Oh, stop these dates," said Penelope. "I want to know what you felt about Oxford."

"Right," I said. "Where shall we start?"

"With your occupation of this house, naturally."

"Well, I was in the peculiar position of a man who loved his home returning to it and finding it in the hands of foreigners, himself an outcast. I had been something of a person in my day. Blues mattered. It was in the days of hero-worship when jobs like governing the Sudan were handed out on a plate to you solely because you were a Blue. I came back to an Oxford where every shop assistant was a Pole or Czech, to streets thronged with workers from Cowley with too much money to spend and no manners. The colleges were mere skeletons of their former selves and had been in some instances taken over by Ministries of one sort or another, to a High where 5-ton trucks, 60-foot lorries, motor coaches, and other vehicles were destroying all the colleges on both sides of the road.

"I used to accompany Jill on her shopping expeditions. No shopkeeper would send anything. We had to traipse in wind and rain, snow and sleet on our bicycles, which were stolen if you didn't lock them, and even then someone stole my saddle. In every shop it was a question of repeating my name over and over again. No one had ever heard of it.

"'Mais—M-A-I-S—S for Sugar,' I used to bleat from behind Jill's shoulder. They couldn't get it right even then.

"There were shops where I used to pay by cheque. Every time the assistant would say, 'Your name and address on the back.'

"And I would write:

S. P. B. Mais (S for Sugar),<br>
291 Woodstock Road,<br>
Oxford.

"We stood in endless queues in the cold, draughty market waiting for fish which was sold out before we reached the slab, the shops with whom we were registered making it clear that it was only because of their courtesy and kindness that we were able to procure any food at all."

"Why did you have to trail round with Jill?"

"Because I was lost without her. I always was, and always shall be. I used to pace up and down outside Blackwell's for hours together, waiting for her, the whole of life passing me by."

"You could have gone inside and looked at the books."

"No! That's just what I couldn't do. Books were pouring out from every publisher. Books were booming. Fortunes were being made, but not by me. My pen had dried up. I couldn't write at all. I kept on getting letters from Hutchinsons reminding me that I was missing the market and the golden opportunity at last to make good. Oxford had made me sterile."

"Oxford?"

"I think so. The lack of sun. The crowds. The foggy, damp, enervating climate. Knowing nobody."

"But surely the society of Oxford was much more satisfying than that of Shoreham?"

"It would have been if I had known anybody. I didn't. I thought that I was going to be asked to High Table at Christ Church. I was invited once, by a doctor who had been up with me. They soon made me realize that I was no longer one of them.

"Occasionally an undergraduate society honoured me by asking me to give them a talk. I remember telling the English Society that the English was a Bastard School. I remember Lord Pakenham founding a club to discuss educational problems and I gave them a talk in which I began by saying that my mother said that compulsory free education was responsible for most of our modern evils. If you want to know what I felt and feel about Oxford we'd better take things as they happened. After all, I've lived here for ten years. We came for ten weeks. Ten years is quite a slice out of one's life.

"On 6th February, 1942, as I told you, I began teaching at Radley. I'd like to draw a veil over that. Bicycling seven miles each way in all weathers. Not able to teach when I got there. Jill seeing me off at the bus-stop when I couldn't bicycle, usually in tears, so much had Oxford got her down. It got us both down. I couldn't have believed that climate could possibly make so much difference."

"It wasn't altogether the climate. You'd lost your home."

"And my income. I was paying £150 a year rent for Toad Hall, which was of course standing empty. I was also paying six guineas a week for this furnished semi-detached villa. I had to find the school fees for Lalage and Imogen. I had to pay Nanny's wages and board as well as that of three others."

"Three others?"

"Yes. Jill had a girl friend who came to live with us and helped with the cooking. She got a job in Oxford. Then an old Nanny of the children came with her young daughter."

"You seem to have had a surfeit of women. I wonder where you put them all."

"There were seven all told. We put Markham and her daughter, Elsie, up in the top nursery, where they had to endure the noise of water dripping in the cistern all night.

"Then there was Nanny, who suffered from some kind of nervous disease, and Diana, who had a bad heart but was so indomitably cheerful and energetic that no one would guess it. She worked in the hospital."

"But why on earth did you, having no money, entertain this crowd?"

"We were always away broadcasting. Someone had to look after the children. It wasn't as if we had any friends. The other half of our semi-detached villa was occupied by Professor Elton, who was ageing rapidly. We had two cats, Tigger and Tim, of whom Imogen was passionately fond. We also had a Corgi called Petal who bit the postman and had to be given away.

"I've always wanted a bulldog, or at any rate a French bulldog, but Jill wanted a Cairn to replace Petal, so I bought her a Cairn which we called Simon. He barks when anybody approaches the house. Not that we got any callers. The newspaper boy and the postman at the front door and the milkman and dustman at the back door were our only contacts with the outside world except for the Nuns."

"The Nuns? I didn't know you were a Catholic."

"I'm not. As my mother was a Petre you'd have expected me to be one, but we're recusants. I used to attend Mass at the Catholic church until the Father took a dislike to something I said. Then I went back to the Established Church, but I don't go to church often in Oxford."

"Your religion. What is it?"

"What I do with my loneliness, worship of the stars by night and the sun, and—oh yes, the wind (which Jill hates) by day. As a small boy I was very devout and believed everything that I was taught."

"And now?"

"I believe in the divinity of Christ. I worship the aristocracy."

"Some people call that snobbery."

"It is snobbery. I am always talking about my own ancestors, the Petres. I use their coat of arms as a bookplate. I'm very proud of having known Edward VIII, Lord Eustace Percy, the Duke of this and the Earl of that, and most of all of having been honoured by the friendship of Sir Norman Birkett, under whose influence I am writing *Buffets and Rewards*——"

"You sound just like your mother."

"I am exactly like my mother in looks and in outlook; like her I'm not intelligent, but curious and dependent on affection. Boys have loved me, but boys grow up and forget. Not many men love me. My greatest friend, Sir Douglas McNair, sees me about once in ten years."

"You'd have liked a title yourself?"

"I'm about the only House man of my generation who is not dead who has escaped either inheriting or earning a title. There's Sir Nelson Rycroft, Sir John Stainton, Sir Wintringham Norton Stable, Lord Halsbury, Lord Birkenhead, and there's a strange private club to which I belong whose members include Lord Verulam, Lord Victor Seymour, Lord Stavordale, the Earl of Westmeath, Lord Phillimore, Lord Portal, Lord Sackville, the Earl of Malmesbury, Viscount Lewisham, Lord Dunglass, Lord Hastings, Viscount Castlereagh, Lord Apsley, Lord Weymouth and Lord David Cecil. I revel in the society of the famous, whether they're artists, authors, actors or politicians. One of my greatest friends is Sir Osbert Sitwell. I should love to have been Sir Petre Mais (S for Sugar), Bart. It goes with a swing."

"Lord Petre Mais goes better."

"Mm. Perhaps so. I'd be content with a baronetcy. I think I shall put in to be created Baron Woodstock."

"Are you seriously suggesting that you've no friends in the Woodstock Road?"

"I didn't make any for the first five years, and five years is a long time. Now of course the house is packed out with undergraduates who come to see Lalage. She's twenty and perhaps the loveliest girl in Oxford.

"The telephone rings all day and night. It's always for her. I like undergraduates. Well, one can only be young once."

"That's rubbish. You've been young all your life. You'll be young when you go to your grave."

"Thank you. I was telling you about my friends, or lack of friends. There's Westerby. She's a dear. She runs a girls' school and Jill and I have tea with her every Sunday. You realize that Jill and I are inseparable. Most men escape from their homes each morning at 8.17 or so and come back at 7.27 or so. My office is my home, my home is my office. It has its advantages. It has its disadvantages. I am liable to interruptions at any moment.

"We go out every day for luncheon to the Kemp. That's a cafeteria. We talk very little, because then Jill is working out her shopping list. I trail round with her after luncheon and we walk round the Meadows and have tea at the Cadena.

"In the evenings when I'm not reviewing a book or play I go to sleep. Jill types. In bed we have little or no communication because Jill invariably reads and I go straight to sleep. I wake up at two or three and get up at once. She sleeps on.

"So it is really only on Sunday afternoons from 4.30 to 6.30 when we go to the Westerbys' for tea that we really get together."

I turned round.

Penelope wasn't there. I heard a cock crow. There were the first faint streaks of dawn away in the east beyond the paddock.

There was the usual slight dent on the settee, and the usual faint scent.

# CHAPTER VII

## OXFORD (1942)

"WE haven't got very far with your adventures in Oxford," said Penelope. "Sorry I had to run away in the middle."

"Run?" I queried.

"Fly, then. You're always so exact."

"I started teaching at Radley. The English master who had got me the job introduced me to the Sixth. 'You're going to have a real intellectual treat,' he began, 'with Mr. Mais. No other schoolmaster of his time has done more to rouse enthusiasm for reading. . . .' Whatever flicker of interest they might have taken in me had I been left to myself died on the instant. From that moment I was doomed.

"How could these boys have heard of me? They weren't born when I was last a schoolmaster. Quite rightly they weren't going to be infused with enthusiasm.

"So far I sympathized. I have never met a nicer lot of boys. But they certainly didn't fall under my spell."

"I expect it was the cold that got you down at Radley."

"Maybe. I've certainly got a 'thing' about heat. I also taught at the Dragon. These small boys were certainly enthusiastic. They crowded round to borrow books. They listened. They argued. I haven't often enjoyed anything more than those Friday afternoons with A1 and 2, and the two form masters who came in at the back, to see, I suppose, that I wasn't lynched. We did have fun."

"You approve of the Dragon?"

"I should say I did. Who could help approving of a school which has turned out men so different as Ronnie Poulton, Charles Fisher, Gaitskell, Joad, J. B. S. Haldane, John Betjeman, Frank Sidgwick, G. L. Cheshire the V.C., and Tom Pakenham?

"I'd put it easily first of English prep schools. But it's very big. I liked it best in 1909 when it had a hundred boys, but it's still got the most vitally alive senior staff I ever came across, and they're friendly enough. I like being called Petre, so long as it comes naturally. Within a couple of days I was 'Petre' to the lot and still am. That's warm, that's friendly. And I needed warmth. I needed friendliness in those bleak days of 1942.

"I earned £1 a week at the Dragon and £240 a year at Radley.

I got £4 a week for a weekly article on books for *Home Chat*. I was trying to write a spy thriller.

"My only way of escape from the world was at Vincent's."

"Tell me about Vincent's."

"As it's an integral part of me I will. I belong to one club in London and one only, as I told you, the Sette of Odd Volumes, whose motto is *Dulce est disipere in loco* and whose members are, in the main, literary:

"We're Poets, Savants, Painters: we're Authors now and then;
We're Doctors, Critics, Scientists, we all are Bookish Men.

So runs 'The Lay of the Odd Volumes'. In point of fact today we seem to have more than a sprinkling of lawyers—G. D. Roberts, Norman Birkett, Moir, Russell Vick, Peter Cadbury, Edgar Lustgarten and a lot more.

"I am glad of that leaven, because I have noticed that lawyers are the most warm-hearted, the most generous and the most friendly of all my Odd colleagues. Before I became a member of the Sette I always regarded judges as inhuman. I never in my wildest moments imagined that the time would ever come when I should find it *dulce desipere in loco* with them.

"Vincent's is a very different club.

"There are two inanimate possessions that I prize more than any others in the world. One is the bronze medal that I wear in the lapel of my dress coat at Odd Volume dinners, which proclaims that I am a member of the Sette. I'll draw it for you. It's like this."

I went over to the settee, caught a whiff of the lovely scent and drew it for her.

"The other is the dark blue tie adorned with silver crowns which proclaims that I am a member of Vincent's Club, Oxford. I have never seen Freddy Grisewood or John Snagge wear any other tie. I never wear any other tie.

"I am proud to belong to the Sette of Odd Volumes, not because it means that I am a writer of any consequence. I am not. It means, if it means anything, that I am thought capable of conviviality and geniality, that I am a good companion.

"I am equally proud to belong to Vincent's, which is not a literary club, for the same reason. Vincent's is mainly composed of Blues, the outstanding athletes of their time. It is true that I was a Blue, but the reverse of outstanding: what fame I attained on the track was not enviable. I am the only man in the history of Inter-University athletics to have fallen down twice in the Three-Mile Race.

"It is not essential for a member of Vincent's to be a Blue or even, if Rule 23 means anything, an athlete. Rule 23 runs: 'That every member of the University may be a candidate for admission after his first year of residence.'

"It is certainly exclusive in the sense that there are 6,000 or more junior resident members of the University, whereas the number of members of Vincent's is limited to 120.

"I was elected to Vincent's over forty years ago. It is perhaps the one place in Oxford that has scarcely changed in spirit at all throughout those troublous memorable years.

"Members still talk earnestly about times on the track, conditions on the river, the state of the wicket, things that don't matter a hoot, or don't they?

"We all know that things are not as they were. We all know that the Oxford of 1909 is a golden dream. Those of us who are not lunatics deplore that. We were carefree. I see no possible advantage in wearing a hair shirt if you can wear a silk shirt.

"I am not a wholesale *laudator temporis acti*. There was a lot that was wrong with those days. The underdogs were many, and the crumbs that fell from their masters' tables were few and more or less accidental. The world, not only of Oxford, has changed, and on the whole very much for the worse. We move faster. Is there any advantage in speed? In the days of the horse-trams I was able to cross The High without risk.

"I find myself completely bewildered by this word 'progress'. To me it stinks, as do most of the words that fall so glibly from the lips of politicians—'co-operation', 'unilateral', 'ceiling', 'target', 'appeasement' and the rest.

" 'Progress' to me means cars that destroy walkers and cyclists, 'pre-fabs', 'Communism', 'Socialism', 'Existentialism', 'Surrealism'. . . .

"I'm in no hurry. As an athlete (of a sort) I have long ago discovered that Father Time can skip along faster the older he gets, and I don't like Time when he's out to defeat the jet aeroplane.

> "Time, you old gipsy man,
> Will you not stay,
> Put up your caravan
> Just for one day?

"What is this life, if full of care
We have no time to stand and stare?

"In my day undergraduates would stand and stare at the passing of the Olympian. Today Blues are no less worthy of hero-worship. Hofmeyer and Martin Donnelly, the New Zealander who had a batting average of nearly 100, walk the streets unnoticed. Your Blue has had his day. I can't imagine why he is in eclipse.

"When I went down from Oxford I was offered a job in the Sudan, solely because I was a Blue. I elected to become a public-school master. I had no difficulty in attaining my ambition, not because I was a scholar—I wasn't—but because I was a Blue. Blues, in 1909, mattered. In 1951 they don't. There's something wrong here. I wasn't much of a chap, but it was a sweat running over Shotover in wind and rain over sticky plough. My contemporary, Noel Chavasse, was sick, I mean sick, every time he ran 100 yards. Noel was killed getting his V.C. I still think that a V.C. matters.

"I'm back to my point about courage being the premier virtue. Faint heart never won fair lady. Faint heart gets you nowhere either in love or war.

"Perhaps you now see why I am so proud to belong to Vincent's and flaunt that blue tie with silver crowns. It means that I believe in guts. Mine have turned to water many a time, but not always. There have been moments when I have been called upon to run and to go on running when my body has given out, times when I've been called upon to go on living when I had nothing to live for. There is a link between physical, mental and spiritual effort. I know quite a bit about physical effort. Did I not pass out, I thought for the last time, on the top of Braeriach, alone? Did I not—but why do I rack my brains and memory to recall instances where I have shown endurance, the capacity to stick things out?

"I must have had guts once or I should certainly not have enjoyed myself so much on that summer afternoon in the dressing-tent at Clay Cross and that winter evening in my rooms in College with the two bowler-hatted gentlemen from Manchester. I've told you about the bookie at Clay Cross.

"The two bowler-hatted gentlemen came as a complete surprise.

" 'What's thee goin' to do, lad, when tha's done wi' Oxford?' asked the first.

" 'I've never given it a thought,' I replied.

" 'Wouldst 'a like a job i' Manchester?'

G

" 'Not much.'

" 'Starting at £300 a year.'

"This was much too good to be true.

" 'Oh well,' I said, 'that's different. What sort of a job?'

" 'We'll find summat as'll suit thee in t' works.'

" 'But what about my qualifications? Why pick on me?'

" 'Tha runs for Derby County?'

" 'I do. What's that got to do with it?'

" 'Thar't too good for Derby. Thee'll run for us i' future, sithee. We're champions, and we're going to stay champions.'

"That encounter ended in a rough house. I was very rude, and they were by no means averse to a rough-and-tumble, though they seemed surprised that I took such a rooted objection to them.

"As a result I always ran much better against their club than before.

"It isn't always, or indeed often, that I have had the courage to suffer physically or financially for my convictions. These were red-letter days to reassure me that I was not wholly contemptible.

"I used to hover about the hall every morning waiting for the postman to bring me replies to the hundreds of letters I had written applying for jobs. The postman always passed our house. So did a dreadful scrubby shuffling tramp who kept his eyes fixed on the ground. He shuffled past every day. One day I took pity on him and gave him my overcoat. He didn't thank me. He didn't put it on. I never saw it again. Whenever I looked up I saw him passing. I used to shut my eyes, count five and look up again. If he had gone, I should get a job. He never had gone. He was always there; me, but for the grace of God. . . . I found myself getting more and more superstitious.

"I felt like a rat in a cage, and often thought of returning to Toad Hall at least to die fighting: to be snuffed out quickly. I found myself writing about ten words, getting up and patrolling the house like a wolf behind bars. I couldn't concentrate. I couldn't think. I felt that I was going mad, and was quite unable to jockey myself out of my appalling lethargy.

"I was asked by the Intelligence Department of the Geographical Survey School to write a history of the Congo. Had I been fit I should have leaped at it, but in my doldrums the effort was too great.

"When I was at my lowest I had a caller. He turned out to be a beggar, who pretended that he had known my father, and I, who couldn't even pay my housekeeping bills, gave him a shilling.

"Every Sunday at noon I got in the habit of riding on my bicycle to the Trout.

"If you know Oxford you can't help knowing the Trout. It is a picturesque Cotswold stone house with peacocks strutting on the roof, with a noisy weir in front of the terrace, a rickety wooden bridge leading to a garden that is islanded between the cut and the weir and remarkable for the most outrageous stone lion in the world, whose enormous stone tail is about the length of a parallel bar. It always incites rude comments from the sober, and scurrilous jokes from those who are less steady on their feet, but wittier.

"I go to the Trout less to drink than to meet one of the most lovable characters in Oxford. This is 'Ma' Coleman, who bears a remarkable resemblance to my mother. I don't know 'Ma' Coleman's age, but it is enough to make me almost idolatrous in my admiration for her energy and vitality. I don't mean her romantic attachment to American colonels who fly from the ends of the earth for five minutes of her electrifying conversation. I don't mean her cooking, which has to be tasted to be believed. I love her for her capacity to fly over to Paris for a couple of hours to attend a wedding. I love her for a merry twinkle in the eye, which completely disarms all who gather round her bar.

"Her patrons are a strangely mixed bag. A large contingent come by charabanc from Birmingham to fish the Thames bank. They sing more than talk. There is a large assortment of Oxford business men bearing names that have been held in high esteem in the city for generations. As it is Sunday they sport deerstalkers, yellow scarves, hunting breeches and thumb-sticks.

"If you were to poke your nose into that overcrowded low-beamed room with the immense open fireplace you'd probably think that you'd chanced on a meet of otter hounds.

"They talk horse and hound, fish and feather. Some of them drive over in gigs, some ride stout grey mares. They own bicycle shops, printing presses and garages. There is also a sprinkling of surgeons from the Radcliffe, dentists, journalists, and, of course, always the actors from the New Theatre.

" 'Ma' Coleman is known to and loved by almost every well-known actor and film star in the country. If you are an autograph-hunter you will find the Trout a most profitable hunting-ground.

"I use the Trout as a gauge of my mental health. When I am ill

I daren't go near the place. When I'm well I enter the famous bar jauntily, elbow my way through the vast crowd that are waiting for sandwiches, beer and the rest of it, and wave airily at a lot of faces that I don't know but which seem somehow familiar.

"I like the Trout best when I can prevail upon Jill to leave the Sunday joint uncooked and have sandwiches on the Trout terrace in the sun, as we watch the sparkle on the swirling waters below the weir."

I stopped.

"Forgive my digressing like this. I was going to tell you what happened on 7th March, 1942, the anniversary of my mother's death.

"On the 7th March, 1942 . . ." I began. Hearing a faint rustle I turned round. Penelope had gone. I was getting used to these disappearances.

10998

# CHAPTER VIII

## OXFORD (1942) (*continued*)

"WHERE were we?" I asked.

"7th March, 1942. The anniversary of your mother's death."

"Oh yes! The only bright spot in an absolutely bleak existence was the appearance of Mrs. Shennan. She is a most fascinating and extremely well-read woman, who had the house next door to us at Toad Hall, and like ourselves had migrated to Oxford. She loved the society of people like ourselves, who were up against it. She used to give us lovely little treats, sudden invitations to the theatre, and wonderful dinner parties at her house in Rawlinson Road. She was a dear. I liked her specially because she had a French bulldog called Rusty. I've always wanted a French bulldog, but so long as Jill's got Simon we can't have another dog, so when we go to Mrs. Shennan's just for an hour or two I can pretend that Rusty's my dog. It was a foul period in my life, this. Mentally, in spite of being in Oxford, or because of its climate, I was stagnating. Physically I was all in. I used to sweat, as if I had a feverish cold, both at tea in the Cadena and in the stalls in the theatre, where I couldn't take in what was going on.

"The only thing I was alive to was the singing of the blackbirds and thrushes in the garden. March is usually to me a golden month. I was in a state of paralytic indecision. Ought we to go back to Toad Hall? Bombs were better than this stifling atmosphere. I should be able to do some writing in the pure Sussex air. I could do nothing in Oxford, in spite of repeated injections by the doctor, except sit and moon in St. John's gardens, the loveliness of which I was quite incapable of appreciating while I was in the depths.

"I scanned every advertisement in *The Times* and replied to every one which looked in the least likely, in spite of the fact that I knew that fifty-seven was far too old to start any new enterprise.

"In my spare moments after teaching at Radley and Magdalen College School I used to go round Oxford with Jill looking for somewhere more congenial and less expensive to live. I began working in the Bodleian, but it was suffocatingly hot, and I sweated there as I did in the cafés and the theatre. Joyce Cary, the novelist, was one of the few people in Oxford to give me intellectual stimulus.

He used to have us round to drinks and I used to marvel at his versatility and tremendous nervous energy. He looks just like a leprechaun."

"He writes like a leprechaun," said Penelope. "I love him."

"Anyone with any sensitivity or imagination naturally would," I said. "We nearly took a house in Holywell that overlooked a churchyard, but it was too Brontë-ish. I was in such a state of misery, being unable to concentrate, that I spent hours every day pacing up and down, to and fro across the hall to the dining-room. I thought that I was going mad. After terrible nightmares I would wake up at three o'clock and then find that I couldn't collect my thoughts. They were all chaotic and suicidal. When Jill bicycled into Oxford to do the shopping I would refuse to go in with her, and then as soon as she'd gone get utterly miserable and chase in after her. The crowds were so great that I never found her, and I used to ride the whole length of the Woodstock Road, back into Oxford, back home and back again looking for her and imagining always that she had been run over. She was sometimes an hour later back than I had counted on, and I'd go to the garden gate a hundred times and peer down the road for the first sight of her. I'm as apprehensive of danger for my loved ones as my mother was. She had more reason than I, because my father courted death every time he drove out of the drive gates. He certainly bore a charmed life.

"As the result of taking time off walking along the valley of the Windrush and watching the first swallows of the year, I suddenly picked up again and found that I could work.

"We went back for a holiday to Brighton, and once more made the journey to Toad Hall. We opened the windows and looked round the rooms. I began fingering my beloved books and felt that I had been a fool to run away. We took Lalage to our Brighton dentist, who to my surprise decided to take out seven of her teeth as her mouth was too crowded. She had, of course, to have this done in bed under an anaesthetic at the Old Ship Hotel. We watched German aeroplanes out at sea attacking a large convoy. It was a magnificent sight. We had air-raid warnings all the time. They acted on me as a tonic after the safety and dullness of Oxford. They dropped several bombs, but nothing near enough to worry us. I felt a quite different man in this crystal-clear air with the sea sparkling in the sun. The holiday was all too short, but it did us a world of good and we prayed for peace to come quickly so that we could come home.

"From Brighton I went up to Southport and then Rochdale and Manchester to lecture. The Northerners are not always gifted with good looks, but they are so warm-hearted and hospitable that I always feel immensely cheered by a Lancashire or Yorkshire audience. I had to give a talk to the chemical factory at Runcorn, which is an abomination of desolation to look at and, of course, reeks with horrible gases.

"It was at the end of April that I found myself at Chipping Sodbury when Bath was blitzed. It was an odd thing that the Germans should have given the West Country a rest of thirteen months, which was precisely the length of my absence, and then start up again on the first night of my return. They gave Bath hell for two nights and at Swindon Station, on our way back to Oxford, we ran into a most pathetic crowd of refugees. I remember one old woman, carrying a parrot in a cage, running up and down the platform quite distraught. She had no idea where she was bound for. There were, of course, numbers of people with bandaged heads and limbs. It was about this time that I went to the Labour Exchange to see if they could find me employment. I little thought, when I started those Occupational Clubs for the unemployed in 1931, that the time would come when I, too, should stand in need of some occupation to prevent me from going mad.

"Now that the Germans had started their 'Baedeker' raids on Bath, Exeter, York and Norwich we were pretty sure that Oxford was about to be razed to the ground, but for a reason that has never been explained Hitler never allowed Oxford to be raided. Perhaps he had decided that he would make Oxford his Berchtesgaden after the war. We never knew.

"Lalage at this time was cultivating a complex about expense. She avoided putting her name down for cricket (a game that she adores and is very good at) because she thought that it would be charged extra on the Dragon bill.

"My hair was now turning white very quickly, and Jill's was beginning to be tinged with grey. One or other of us was always running a temperature. Lalage's went up to 103·4° for no reason at all. The school doctor could find nothing wrong with her, so I went to a new man who diagnosed her disease as 'flu. It was such a lovely hot May that I began taking the children in a punt on the Cher. We only paddled, as I haven't punted for years. I wouldn't let the children take out a canoe. I was as ill as that. We played a little tennis. I began going out at night to Bomber Command and other

R.A.F. stations lecturing. I got a guinea a night. I had to do my share of fire-watching, a singularly pointless exercise in view of the fact that Oxford was never raided.

"On one single day I applied for a job on the staff at Eton, to the B.B.C. for a post on the agricultural staff, to the Disabled Soldiers' Educational staff, the Dorset County Educational staff, a big business firm who advertised for a secretary, another big business firm who wanted a Director of Publicity, and a trade journal which advertised for an editor.

"I wasted an enormous amount of time and money on these and similar advertisements and never received a single reply. With my face glued to the window I looked out every morning for the appearance of the postman, but with fiendish regularity he passed by. It is bad enough to find that you are not indispensable when you are young. It is infinitely worse to discover that you are not indispensable and not wanted when you are old and have been a public figure of some consequence.

"When, on leaving the R.A.F., I sought my fortune in Fleet Street, I was interviewed by Lord Beaverbrook.

" 'Where were you educated?' he asked.

" 'Oxford,' I replied proudly.

" 'Forget it,' he said tersely. I did. In order to adapt myself to the standards of Fleet Street I forgot my University. Now—a neat revenge—I had been forgotten by my University. I don't quite know what I expected, recognition of some sort, if not a job ('There must be thousands of jobs going for Oxford men in Oxford,' they said), at any rate an invitation to High Table. I have lived in Oxford ten years. In the whole of that time I have been invited to dine at High Table once in my own college, as I told you, once at Magdalen, New College, All Souls, and Jesus, and twice at Hertford.

"Not that I shone or even much liked it when I was asked. Dons' interests are rarely my interests.

"In all colleges at High Table the food is rich and plentiful, the wine (equally excellent) flows freely. It ought to loosen my tongue. It doesn't. I admire the portraits on the wall which look all the better for being seen dimly by candlelight. I admire the massive silver cups. It is fun going from a protracted meal at High Table to Senior Common Room for port, peaches, crystallized fruits and nuts on a table that glitters in the subdued light, and then on again for coffee and whisky or beer in a cosier room where we break up into different parties. It is fun, but you have to be in the mood for it. I seldom was.

"During the Summer term I used to watch Lalage playing cricket at the Dragon. Like Jill she has a natural aptitude for the game, which is uncommon in girls. Both have got a safe pair of hands and good eyes. I seem to have spent the greater part of that golden summer sleeping, waiting for the post, bathing, playing cricket, drinking beer and repeating in my diary that I had nothing to look forward to but bankruptcy.

I went up to the Pressed Steel Works and was offered a job at £300 a year as a commercial traveller. I didn't take it. I interviewed Lord Brocket, who wanted me to take over the secretaryship of the Land Union, and on the same day Francis Dillon, of the B.B.C., offered me the editorship of a new feature to be called 'Country Magazine'. Of all features on the air this has proved to be the most popular, for it has run for ten years without a break.

"The next day I turned down an offer of £400 a year from the Abingdon Social Centre.

"I spent my fifty-seventh birthday (4th July) playing cricket for the Fathers against the Dragons. I made nine runs.

" 'Country Magazine' went on the air for the first time on 12th July. I got 25 guineas as compère, which I thought a princely rate of pay. All I had to do was to make the country speakers feel at their ease. The half-hour programme was interrupted in the middle with a musical interlude for which Francis Collinson was responsible. Collinson was an affable Scot who was indefatigable in his search for appropriate and authentic folk songs. Dillon was an Irishman with a shock of unruly hair and a high treble voice. We gave our shows in the Grafton Theatre, Tottenham Court Road. It was an honest programme in which listeners heard the authentic voice of the country. We collected farmers, land-girls, poachers, small-holders, boatmen, duck-shooters, carpenters, blacksmiths, all sorts, most of them tongue-tied and inclined to fluff, but most of whom put over a good story, and I am not surprised that they caught the public fancy. It was a fortnightly programme given at 1.10 on Sunday afternoon, obviously a good hour for listening for those who listen at meal-times instead of bickering among themselves. We had no audience at these shows. Such laughter as there was came from our fellow-performers and Collinson's string quartet. The procedure was simple. We all met and ran through the scripts on Saturday morning. We met again at 10 o'clock on the Sunday morning and rehearsed without a break till about 12.50, when we raced across the road to a pub for a pint of beer, which we badly needed.

"A boy in my form went down with infantile paralysis. He recovered and I saw him on Paddington platform shortly afterwards. I leaned out of my carriage window and shouted, 'How's the sleepy sickness?'

"An admiral sitting next to me in the compartment sprang up like a frightened hare. 'Do I understand,' he said to me, 'that you have been in contact with sleepy sickness?'

" 'Certainly, sir,' I said, 'there's the victim. I'm his form-master. He looks well on it, doesn't he?'

"The admiral retired to another compartment.

"I was tremendously pleased at the end of that Summer term to find that Lalage at the age of eleven came third in the Open School Diving Competition. She is a quite fearless and very neat diver.

"We spent August in a small hotel in Ilfracombe. It was packed full of trippers and rained almost every day. Crowds stood nightly on the Capstone singing 'You Are My Sunshine'. My only relief was the Britannia bar.

"The trouble with Ilfracombe is the lack of sand and the number of visitors. The country round is attractive enough, and as it is near the home of my childhood I naturally think highly of North Devon. We went over by bus to Woolacombe to bathe, but there were red flags warning us off and guns banging all the time. We had to queue for an hour for the bus to take us to Woolacombe and another hour in the afternoon for a bus to take us back to Ilfracombe. As it rained practically all and every day it wasn't much of a holiday, though Jill found compensations in the shops. The children enjoyed the bathing and were angry when I kept them out of the water if it was raining. There was nothing else for them to do, for there is no level ground in Ilfracombe where you can play games.

"I had to go up to London to broadcast the 'Country Magazine' programmes, something of an ordeal in war-time's overcrowded trains, but worth it for the sake of the 25 guineas. Besides, I liked being in the programme, even though I didn't have to say much beyond introducing the speakers.

"I remember passing the school at Templecombe on the way up on Saturday, and on the way back on Sunday it wasn't there. The Germans had destroyed it in the night.

"We went back to Oxford after a month, and I then had to go

to London to give a fresh series of 'Kitchen Front' broadcasts. I gave six of these talks on six successive days and then went off to Bristol to give a 'Country Magazine' programme from there. I then went back to Radley and Magdalen College School for a day or so and then up to Derbyshire to prepare a 'Country Magazine' talk. I got a farmer, a quarryman, a mill-hand, a mole-catcher and a carpenter.

"I used to get a guinea for taking Overseas troops round the colleges. It took up a tremendous amount of time, but the Americans in particular seemed to like it. I usually confined myself to Christ Church, Merton and Magdalen.

"In October I started a series of broadcast talks to America. These took place at 2 a.m. from 200 Oxford Street, and my chief was George Orwell, who was desperately ill and naturally lugubrious. I liked him very much, but he didn't like life. I gave lectures on how to keep warm at Dorland House for the Ministry of Food. I lectured to Bomber Command on Shakespeare. At a given point I had to leave the car and be blindfolded lest I should know its exact locality.

"On Allhallowe'en I went up to Scotland for a Scottish number of 'Country Magazine', which was great fun.

"On my return I went on giving my American broadcasts, which tired me so much that I had to refuse an invitation to take part in a debate in the Union. I was then asked to broadcast to New Zealand. All the talks to Overseas were simple descriptions of our daily life in England. I found time to give a talk on 'Words' to the High School, Oxford. I had also to go to Chelmsford to open a Fuel Exhibition there.

"I wrote a radio feature programme called 'Mermaid in the Zodiac', which I read to the Dragon. The idea was to put up a Cambridge team of Tudor poets against an Oxford team. I was invited to go on to 'Youth Magazine'. There was one day towards the end of the year when I broadcast to the United States at two in the morning, took the chair at Foyle's Luncheon, rehearsed a New Zealand talk and a 'What I'm Reading Now' talk to schools. I also recorded a 'Country Magazine' talk. I broadcast to America on Christmas Eve and I see from my diary that I described Christmas Day as the best I had ever spent. As we dined with Mrs. Shennan, I think I can see the reason for that entry.

"At any rate we finished the year in good style by going off to Brighton, which always puts me back in favour with God and man."

# CHAPTER IX

## OXFORD (1943)

"AND SO," said Penelope, "we come to 1943."

"1943—it seems so infinitely far away. I can remember nothing about it. I can remember my childhood vividly. The older I get the more clearly I can remember all sorts of incidents of youth, but 1943? No. I shall have to refer again to my diary.

"We were in Sussex for the New Year, and was I glad to be home again?

"We followed hounds on foot, picked catkins, went over to have a look at Toad Hall and I prepared broadcast talks to New Zealand.

"I remember being asked to open Southwick's Civic Restaurant.

"I came back here to go on struggling at Radley and Magdalen College School. I went down with 'flu. I used to get 'flu regularly every year. I caught it from my form at Radley, who were also down with measles and mumps. The Lent term ought to be abolished. I went on broadcasting to America, started yet another series of 'Kitchen Front' talks, and gave more 'Country Magazine' programmes.

"Lalage and Imogen were together at the Dragon that Summer term, and I used to spend long afternoons watching them play cricket and bathing.

"I earned an unexpected panegyric in *The Listener*. That was in May. Here it is:

"There are other old-timers, whose consistent excellence too often passes unchronicled. S. P. B. Mais, for instance. There he was the other night, nonchalantly turning up to give a book talk on 'What I'm Reading Now", and making as good a job of it as he can of a dozen other assignments. He has an uncommon skill for reviewing a book in a couple of sentences, and he manages to convey not only a digest of the book's content but also a bold impression of its flavour. His criticism is all the more interesting, to my mind, because it is so often partisan. Mais takes sides, but whether you like his recommendations or not you cannot fail to be impressed by the ardour and the integrity which he puts into his judgments. He is very much at home at the microphone. There is no complacency about his manner, no manipulation of tricks; only the unobtrusive confidence of a man who has the measure of his medium. Mais is not a show-piece, he is a first-class adult.

"I treasure that. The writer was E. A. Williams."

"Obviously a man of discernment."

"It was the same week that I was taken off the 'Country Magazine' programme. That's the way my life works. In order to keep myself occupied I started a novel. I first of all called it *All Change*. Ultimately it became *Caper Sauce*."

"Autobiographical?"

"Of course. All my novels are autobiographical. It was just about this time that we found we could lease the house unfurnished at £100 a year instead of furnished at six guineas a week, as we'd been paying up till then. We paid one of our periodic visits to Toad Hall in July and found that it had become an officers' mess. We spent practically the whole of a baking July day going through our furniture, which was in store in an empty house in The Drive. We hadn't room in this semi-detached villa for more than a small fraction of the stuff we had amassed through the years. I had to sell thousands of volumes of books that were very precious to me. There were two men in charge of the furniture. One stuttered and the other got the numbers that we told him to take down of the items we wished to have sent to Oxford mixed up with those we wished to sell. As we had had the hell of a haggle over each piece before we decided on its fate, that didn't improve our tempers. Possessions are odd things. I find that I put things in the bottom of a drawer and forget them for years and then discover that I want them every day. That's specially true of the watches that I collect. I've got a mania for wrist-watches."

"And first editions."

"And yellow silk handkerchiefs."

"And notebooks."

"And diaries."

"And sinister-looking knives."

"And snuff-boxes."

"And now a monocle. You are a child."

"Well, I share that quality with Pepys. I think it's a good one."

"So long as you can afford to indulge it."

"Isn't it true that luxuries are really the only necessities? Silk pyjamas, funny caps, ski-ing jerseys."

"You must have found it difficult to know which things to select if you act on the principle that only luxuries are essential."

"That Summer is memorable as Removal Summer. We had the devil of a time getting our stuff up from Brighton.

"The people who owned the furniture in our house suddenly decided that they were going to take it away before the end of July. We had fixed to go to Woolacombe on the 24th. I remember that there was a terrific heat-wave and I was feeling like death, anyway. I wasn't doing any good at Radley.

"We sent off our advance luggage on the 26th and on the 27th saw all the furniture that we had been using taken out of the house. Our furniture was due to arrive by road from Brighton on the 28th. On that day we were told that there was a delay and that it was coming by rail. Imogen, Lalage and I spent the whole day at the garden gate looking for the arrival of the pantechnicons which never came. I was specially resentful because the weather was perfect for Woolacombe beach and unbearable in the Woodstock Road.

"On the 30th—it was the Friday before Bank Holiday—there was still no furniture, and I decided not to wait any longer but to take Lalage and Imogen on to Ilfracombe. Jill was to follow as soon as the container with the furniture arrived.

"We had an appalling journey. In order to avoid the crowds we took the 7.10 to Paddington, and there found ourselves in the middle of a maelstrom. We stood for hours on the crowded platform, and when the train came in the carriage doors were locked.

"We did, however, sit down, and at 1.20 had got as far as Taunton. Then followed an agonizing five hours in a slow train that had stood in a siding in the baking sun for hours before it started.

When eventually we got to Ilfracombe both the children were ill.

"The next day we queued for the bus to Woolacombe, where we were met by notices in the shop windows, 'No buns for non-residents.'

"I kept on telephoning to Oxford to see if the furniture had arrived.

"The children were easy enough to cope with, but they missed Jill. So did I. I fussed too much over the risks of their falling off rocks and catching chills.

"The hotel was unbearably full. There was nowhere to sit except in our sunless back bedroom. The crowds were like locusts, eating up all the sweets and chocolates. I remember seeing a notice, 'Feeding the gulls is a legal offence.' The heat-wave broke. The rains came and we had to spend our days in shelters.

"It wasn't until we had been there a week that I got a telegram from Jill: 'Last load arrived 9 a.m. Coming tomorrow.'

"I got her on the telephone and she sounded quite delirious with joy to have got the furniture in at last.

"On the day that she arrived, the 7th of August, Lalage fell sick and had to stay in bed. We met three trains before the one that brought Jill. At dinner we drank a bottle of Moet and Chandon. We only drink champagne at Christmas, so you can realize how important the occasion was.

"Jill had missed the heat-wave and arrived in Ilfracombe when there was nothing whatever to do except try to keep out of the icy wind and rain. The fog siren booming on Bull Point did nothing to make us more cheerful.

"We managed to put in a few walks over the cliffs to Lee, where we found an unexpectedly good place to have luncheon. Jill was happy because there were plenty of shops. I had no alternative but to trail round in her wake.

"I was depressed and sleepless because I had no work at all except one weekly article for *Home Chat*.

"Imogen, who was only six years old, walked eight miles with us one day over the cliffs and appeared to like it. She is more interested in birds and flowers than Lalage, who gets much more quickly bored.

"On Imogen's seventh birthday (12th August) we had a grand day bathing at Woolacombe, and at night we opened another bottle of champagne.

"We went to Barnstaple Market, but all I remember is the queue waiting for the bus to go in and the queue waiting for the bus to bring us back. Jill had more fun than I did. She picked up an unexploded shell on the beach and brought it back to the hotel.

"A neighbour, David Whittaker, had come down with us. He spent the day singing 'I Am Your Sunshine' till I could have strangled him. My only refuge was the bar in the Britannia at night and on the sands at Woolacombe by day when it was fine.

"On our last Sunday I went up to the churchyard to have a look at my grandfather's grave. He died at the age of ninety-six. I read there that his father was Harry Mais of Kingston, Jamaica, and that my lovely grandmother, Warne, was daughter of a Dean of Exeter who had been at Harrow with Byron.

"On that particular Sunday Lalage's cough was so bad that she had to come out of church.

"If only it hadn't rained all and every day! I met a woman in the Britannia who said, 'This is the first holiday I've had for five years and I've just got to drink to forget the rain.' I can't think why we spend our holidays in such a climate."

"You didn't, later."

"I didn't, later. But what years I wasted in English seaside resorts where there was nothing better to do than count the drops of rain as they dripped down the window-pane of the bedroom! No wonder we take to drink. If it does nothing else, drink does warm one. My bill for that holiday came to just under £100. I should have been happier if I'd stayed in Oxford.

"After the final ritual of washing our hands in the sea we took train for Oxford, and were delighted to be among our own *lares and penates* once more. The delight was slightly modified by the sight of moths all over the place, and huge spiders which always send Lalage into hysterics.

"As soon as we left the sea the weather improved. We celebrated our return with a chicken and a bottle of Beaujolais.

" 'Only by drinking,' I wrote in my diary, 'can I drown the awful miasma that has overtaken me.'

"I should have liked the house more if I had not been horrified of having a nervous breakdown owing to my inability to find a job. I was also worried over Lalage's cough.

"I took her to a doctor, who diagnosed pneumonia and told me that I ought to have brought her at least a fortnight earlier. He put her on M & B. I had to go up to London to broadcast on the series 'Transatlantic Call' on the day of her crisis. Luckily her temperature fell and I went off to Southport to lecture in a happier frame of mind; which, however, was dissipated when I got the bill for removing my furniture from Brighton. It was £180.

"I found teaching at Radley in that Autumn term a terrible strain. As soon as Lalage got over her pneumonia Imogen went down with it. You can guess how miserable I was from this entry: 'It's beastly to be like this. People begin to hate you, forgetting the man you once were and only remembering the wreck. Far better die when one is on the crest of the wave, than live in this disgusting, fumbling, fantastic way, a nuisance to everyone, with a deteriorating mind and disintegrating body. It's a frightful effort for me even to write this diary.' "

"Well, it's a bit steep to have both your children down with pneumonia. Enough to get anybody down."

"I was down all right. Lalage was in tears because she wasn't in the Dragon play. I was irritable. I had an awful job fighting for a place on the train when I went up to Broadcasting House to do a series called 'Answering You'.

"Things were just about at their lowest when Jill's Corgi, Petal, bit the postman and we had a grand row. We got out of it by giving the dog away to a woman in Headington, who apparently liked the idea of a dog that bit postmen.

"Then out of the blue came an offer. I was walking down the Haymarket when an old pupil of mine at Tonbridge in naval uniform accosted me and told me that Admiral Denis Boyd, the Fifth Sea Lord, wanted me to take over the Cultural Activities of the Fleet Air Arm. I had an interview with Boyd, who was full of enthusiasm for this project, as was I. It was Cranwell all over again. I went down to see the Admiral in Command, Robinson, at Lymington, and we went through the whole thing and I was all agog. At last a job at £1,000 a year, and just when I was getting used to the idea the Admiralty clamped down on it and said that they couldn't afford it.

"It's not easy, looking back, to realize just how shattered I was. The carrot in front of the donkey's nose had been taken away. The only cheerful thing was that Lalage did, after all, get a place in the chorus of the Dragon play, *The Pirates of Penzance*.

"Just before Christmas I made my one and only appearance on the Brains Trust with Lord David Cecil, Julian Huxley and George Gibson. There was only one question that I could tackle and that was on girls' christian names. I'm not surprised that I was never asked again.

"That brings us to the end of 1943, summarized by me in my diary as 'The worst year of my life by a million miles.' "

# CHAPTER X

## OXFORD (1944)

"WAS it the truth," asked Penelope, "to describe 1943 as the worst year of your life?"

"Factually, perhaps not. Imaginatively, yes. It was all high temperatures and low spirits."

"And yet you were doing what you like best in the world, teaching."

"That's just the point. It was the year in which I discovered that I could no longer teach. The old magic touch had gone."

"Isn't it just on the cards that that was only temporary?"

"No! I've staged a come-back in books. I can still write, but teaching, like broadcasting, is a thing of the past for me."

"So long as you've got your public platform and can express what you want to put over, why worry?"

"I don't. It was in 1943 that I was worrying."

"What about 1944?"

"I began well by reviewing books for the *Oxford Mail*. This has been my stand-by for the last seven years. I like reviewing books. For one thing it means that I no longer have to buy so many new books. It enables me to keep abreast of what's going on in poetry, fiction and the theatre. It helps me financially, for I sell the books to Blackwell's when I've read them. Unfortunately I have to mark them in pencil pretty lavishly, which reduces the price. Then there is the £4 a week. For a long time that was my only regular salary. I like to review only the books I like. There's no point in calling attention to the second-rate.

"Yes. I like reviewing. I like getting letters from authors whose work pleases me. Dorothy Sayers, Enid Bagnold and Sir Alan Herbert all honoured me by expressing gratitude at what I had said about their work. Authors are much more modest than most people believe."

"You?"

"Me, most of all. I've the most reason to be, because so very little of all my prodigious output has been worth while. I've got terrific energy, but I lack art. I lack the time, I lack the ability to phrase my findings about life memorably. I'm apt to be slipshod, as people in a hurry often are. That's why I like reviewing books. I like watching the proficiency of professionals. My life is, in a sense, all of a piece. I am as enthusiastic a cricketer as any man living, but I just can't play the game. Even Dragon boys can bowl me out. I don't know how to bowl. I field well. I lack technique. I was as keen a player of Rugger as ever lived, but again I lacked technique. I enjoyed the game, but never shone at it."

"What about running?"

"I wasn't quite in the first class even there. I had a superb wind and I ran, as I played cricket and Rugger, by the light of nature. I ride, and love riding, but I've seldom dared to ride to hounds. I can't jump. I ski, and I love ski-ing, but I'm now back to doing kick turns. I dance, I love dancing, but it's only when I wear my monocle or a false beard that I have the courage to try the Samba.

"It's the same with everything that I do in life. I'm a book reviewer, as I told you, but I'm not Sir Desmond McCarthy. I'm a novelist, but I'm not in the same world as Elizabeth Myers, Elizabeth Taylor, or Elizabeth Bowen. I'm the eternal amateur. I know England better than most writers, and I have written more travel books than any other man in England, but it's H. V. Morton that people read when they're in search of England.

"I started 'Country Magazine' in the war, but it's Ralph Wightman who's got the technique that appeals to the great mass of people. I'm always an also-ran."

"But you do run. That's something. You're belittling yourself."

"I don't think so. I'm stating the facts. Energy by itself is not enough. Enthusiasm by itself is not enough."

"They combined to make you a first-rate schoolmaster."

"Not everybody thought so. I can't think of a single thing that I've ever done well."

"As a mathematician you must have read G. H. Hardy."

"What's he got to do with it? You're not going to pretend that I did well in Maths? I took a third in Mods."

"Hardy said, 'It is a tiny minority who can do anything really well, and the number who can do two things well is negligible.'"

"Yes, I remember his saying that, and he followed it up by saying, 'If a man has any genuine talent, he should be ready to make almost any sacrifice in order to cultivate it to the full.'

"I suppose that's the trouble. I've never really sacrificed anything. Let's get back to 1944. We went back to Brighton and stayed at the Dudley in Hove, one of the most luxurious hotels I ever stayed in. We met H. E. Bates there. He's one of the lucky men who can do one thing perfectly. He can write. We also met an Eton master called Pemberton, a historian who also can write well. He wrote a very good book on Cobbett and another on Palmerston. I remember spending the whole of an icy day going through thirty-two cases of my books that I had left in store. I was offered and accepted £151 from Cambridge's for about a thousand books. It cut me to the heart to part with them."

"Why didn't you keep them?"

"No room, and I couldn't afford to anyway. It was difficult trying to decide which to keep and which to throw out. I kept most of my modern poets, sold all my modern fiction, and kept all the topographical stuff that I could. I gave away all the invaluable pamphlets about places that I had collected in my travels. There was a time when I used to give the MSS. of all my books to the Hove Public Library, but I couldn't think that anybody could want them now, so I threw them all away. They took up far too much room. I threw away all my volumes of press-cuttings as well. The London School of Journalism offered me a tutorial job, which I took, and then John Curran, the Cardiff iron and steel magnate, asked me to write the history of his firm. Advertising always pays best. I charge 15 guineas per thousand words, and leave it to the firm to decide on the number of words they want. We went over to Cardiff and spent several days going over the various processes. I found Curran a charming, simple, good-natured Irish Catholic. His nephew, the son of the features editor of the *Evening Standard*, was in my form at the Dragon, a very good boy indeed, with plenty of imagination, who worked hard enough to get a high scholarship into Rugby.

"I was finding Radley more trying than ever. It ate into my time and left me too tired to tackle the novel I was writing, my book reviews, my London School of Journalism pupils and the Curran book. I was still at work on the book about the history of paper, and the Managing Director, Winskill, took us up to Lincolnshire to see a sugar-beet factory at Brigg. I had a theory in my mind about this time that my depression and lethargy were in part due to snuffing, so I stopped and deluded myself into the belief that all my nervous mental disorder was due to the taking of snuff. I have never met a doctor who could find any evidence that snuff is harmful. At any rate I had snapped out of my miasma. I was well enough to dine at High Table at Hertford.

"As soon as I got well Jill went down and became even more

depressed than I had been. I found that I was making a better go of
it with my Radley form. We had a minor excitement in February.
A bevy of waxwings settled in some bushes at the Roundabout,
where the traffic was most congested. Waxwings are supposed to
come only when the weather is going to be exceptionally cold. These
birds, which are like crested thrushes, stayed about three weeks,
and contingents of boys from Radley cycled over to have a look
at them. The Romans regarded them as birds of ill-omen. I wondered
what tragedy their arrival held in store for me.

"In March I went up to Sheffield and Doncaster, sent by the
Ministry of Agriculture to open their 'Dig for Victory' weeks. I
stayed with my cousins, the Fords, at Ilkley. I always like staying
with them because John is a keen fisherman and shot, and takes us
out with him. The country round Ilkley is exciting and invigorating.
I am at my happiest on high moors, crossing Dartmoor to Cranmere,
crossing Ilkley Moor with grouse getting up at my feet all over the
place, or on Haworth Moor in pursuit of the spirit of Emily Brontë."

"Another blithe spirit."

"I'll say she is. She's just as real to me as you are."

"Let's get back to these cousins."

"We went up to Skipton. Somewhere near Appletreewick we
picked up a boy and girl who'd been walking over the fells for
three days. That's the way to forget: But we got a reminder. As we
were crossing Ilkley Moor the next day we were led by the cries of
curlew to a deserted place where we saw all that was left of a
Canadian bomber. The wreckage was whining wistfully in the wind.
I ripped off the altimeter as loot. It was a magnificent Spring, a
time of swallows and kingfishers, early primroses and cowslips.
We cycled all over the Cotswolds, and on 12th April went to
Llanwrtyd for the first time. Llanwrtyd's a tiny fishing village with
an hotel standing right on the river bank. We rode to hounds on the
boggy hills, we saw the hillsides dotted with newly-born lambs.
There were curlew all over the marshes. We were fed like princes.
From the tops of the hills we could see for fifty miles and not a
house anywhere, just fold after fold with the Brecon Beacons and
Carmarthen Van standing sentinel above the lesser, smoother heights.
We were looking for kites, of which there are only about twelve left
in the United Kingdom, and they're all in the Llandovery-Builth
area and well guarded. We rode everywhere and picnicked by the
side of Wolf's Leap, below the deserted Drover's Way near
Abergwesyn.

"We were a gay party. There was Lalage's form master at the Dragon, Tom and Antonia Pakenham, two of the brightest children in the school, and a solicitor, Kenneth Thomas, of Peterhouse, Cambridge.

"After the day's outing we used to meet in the long bar, and over the best beer I ever tasted tell—and listen—to tales of old Wales, the most interesting being that of Twm Shon Catti, the outlaw who lived in a cave at the junction of Cardigan, Carmarthen and Brecon, and who compelled the widow of the farmer at Ystradfin to marry him by threatening to cut off her hand at the wrist if she didn't. We had a hunt breakfast in the kitchen of this farm. There are two ecstasies in this world that carry me right out of myself: riding over an open moor either in pursuit of the fox or not, and ski-ing. Lalage got the brush on one of these hunts and was blooded. Imogen's turn was to come. We saw another crashed aeroplane on the lonely moors to remind us of events elsewhere. I met a girl who showed me a whole lot of mementoes of the Jacobite Secret Societies in the time of Prince Charles Edward. She also told me that the Holy Grail had been taken from Glastonbury at the Dissolution of the monasteries to Strata Florida, and was still on view in a farm called Nant Eos, but that the olive wood of the chalice was now lined with silver because souvenir hunters had been cutting pieces off the wood. The Easter holidays are always lovely, with the coming of the swallow and the cuckoo and the blossoming of violets and primroses.

"I haven't often been asked to talk to undergraduate societies during my ten years in Oxford, but that Summer term the English Club asked me to talk on 'Soldier Poets'. I also lectured to the Wrens. Then the *Daily Express* put me on the panel of their Brains Trust with Commander Campbell, Joad and others. I was paid £75 for appearing on their Brains Trust at Dundee, Perth and Edinburgh.

"The 6th of June, you may remember, was D-Day. Lalage was thirteen on the 15th. I contracted pneumonia on the 16th and found that my reactions to M & B only induced nightmares. While I was ill I had one of the most inane jobs I ever undertook. A firm of printers hired me to write captions for a coloured calendar. Owing to my pneumonia I missed seeing Lalage take the part of the doctor's gentlewoman in the Dragon version of *Macbeth*. I spent my fifty-ninth birthday (4th July) in bed swallowing doses of sulphadiozene. My pneumonia lasted forty-three days, so I lost half a term's salary at Radley.

"On the first day of the Summer holidays an undergraduate rode Imogen down at the crossroads between Holywell and the Broad. I took him into Blackwell's and told him that owing to his stupidity he had probably given the child a complex about bicycles. He had. Never since has she ridden into Oxford without fear.

"On 1st August we went to Porthcawl, the air of which immediately cleared up my congested lung. I had a glorious holiday riding over the sands, playing golf, bathing, surfing, eating, drinking and sleeping. Imogen cut her foot badly as the result of slipping off a rock. Jill dropped a valuable gold bangle in the sea. We had the luck to run into a heat-wave, so we lazed most of every day with little family games of cricket in between bathes. Our high-spot was the discovery of Mrs. Judd of Merthyr Mawr, a village on the other side of the sand dunes. She gave us such a stupendous tea that we formed the habit of going over to her whenever we wanted a walk. We spent seven weeks in Porthcawl and I was enchanted with it. Lalage started her first term at Cheltenham on 20th September. The house felt empty without her. I was quite lost. It was the first time that we had been separated. Luckily I had my work at Radley to occupy my mind.

"Then I got a job at Fraserburgh to write up the history of pneumatic tools. We spent many days inspecting the factory. I got 75 guineas for writing a history of Surrey. I opened a 'Dig for Victory' exhibition at Ilkeston and got a further 100 guineas for writing the history of steel for Peech & Tozer. I had to inspect refractories at Streetly, quarries at Coxhoe, and great tanks at Hartlepool and Harrington. I like doing this sort of work, but it's pretty strenuous getting the technical side right and making it palatable to the general reader. It pays much better than writing ordinary books, but of course there are no royalties. You are paid outright.

"On 23rd October Priscilla flew over from Paris and I immediately telephoned to her. Her voice was sweet, low and staccato, just like a child's.

"After my morning at Radley I used to walk round Christ Church
remembered how as an undergraduate I used to run every morning at seven o'clock. One morning I was accosted by a tubby, cheerful-faced stranger who asked if he might join me. He didn't tell me his name till years afterwards. It was William Temple, later Archbishop of Canterbury.

"At half-term we went down to Cheltenham to see Lalage. She

seemed happy but desperately afraid lest she should be infringing a rule.

"You'll notice that I haven't mentioned broadcasting. For eleven months the B.B.C. ignored me and on 9th November they accepted my script on 'How I Failed to Find a Kite', an account of the Llanwrtyd holiday.

"Priscilla came to stay with us, and she told me that she had spent two months in one concentration camp and then for three and a half years lived on false papers.

"On 8th December I went down with epidemiditis. The doctor suggested that I ought to have my enlarged prostate removed. The surgeon said 'Not yet.' But it meant the end of my day-to-day diary. Like Queen Victoria, I began to keep a diary when I was thirteen, and I kept it up all through my school and University days.

"I shall never keep a diary again. I had followed Johnson's advice to Boswell: 'He recommended me to keep a journal of my life, full and unreserved. He counselled me to keep it private.'

"If Johnson could have had the privilege of seeing Boswell's diary he would have had the shock of his life to discover how well he had obeyed the injunction to keep it full and unreserved. It is the most unreserved diary in the world. Johnson told him to put down everything that happened to him. 'The great thing to be recorded is the state of your own mind, and you should write down everything that you can remember, for you cannot judge at first what is good or bad: and write immediately while the impression is fresh, for it will not be the same a week afterwards.'

"I'm afraid mine wasn't so candid as his. At school it was a record of runs made at cricket, money borrowed and Holy Communions celebrated. As it's almost wholly illegible I've never been able to read much of it even if I'd wanted to, and I've never wanted to.

"I can't imagine why Boswell didn't obey Johnson's precept and keep it private. He bequeathed it to his nephews and nieces. It's perhaps as well that they never saw it. Pepys was a Quaker compared with Boswell. Do you keep a diary?"

"Women don't keep diaries."

"Lalage does. She keeps three concur̶r̶e̶n̶t̶ ̶.̶ ̶.̶ ̶.̶ ch to put in them except a record of the cocktail parties she has attended. I don't think that my diary has helped my autobiography much. It has served to remind me of certain facts, but in a good autobiography you don't want facts, or if you use facts they're there just to make a character clearer. For the rest of my autobiography I shall rely on my imagination for my facts."

"It's more entertaining that way."

"I'm at least as likely to reveal my real self that way. I don't reveal anything much by repeating that the children are running a temperature, or that I'm suicidally depressed because of my inability to earn as much as I spend. I have bouts of spending and bouts of saving when I won't turn the radio on, cancel the papers, sit in the dark, walk rather than take a bus, and go to the cheapest seats in the cinema."

Penelope laughed.

"There goes your imagination. You never go to the cheapest seats in the cinema."

"I used to."

"You never did. When you were a boy you used to spend ninepence or a shilling in the gallery of the theatre, but cinemas weren't invented."

"How like a woman to pin me down like that! The principle's the same."

There was no answer. When I turned round she had gone.

# CHAPTER XI

## OXFORD (1945-51)

"AND now," said Penelope, "1945."

"1945, Victory Year. How hollow that sounds now and how little I remember of it. The year began in the worst possible way for me. I was suffering excruciating pain from this attack of epidemiditis.

"We spent the first fortnight of the year at the Old Ship, Brighton, but as I was laid up on a settee in the lounge and couldn't get out into the sunshine it was hell.

"Christopher Stone and Ivor Stewart-Liberty commiserated with me, obviously sure that I should be in my grave in a few weeks. When I got back to Oxford it looked as if I were in for a major operation. Luckily the surgeon decided against it and I got my reprieve.

"I remember going down to Cheltenham at half-term to see Lalage, who seemed happy but found the work very hard.

"In March we went down to Cardiff again for our second tour of Curran's factories to get material for the book on the foundry. At Easter we went back to Llanwrtyd and enjoyed an idyllic fortnight of heat-wave, which meant that we bathed every day in the Yrfon, rode over the hills, listened to the curlew, went in search of the kites, were soothed to sleep by the noise of the river below the bedroom window, ate ravenously, drank a lot and really relaxed.

"In April events moved fast. Hitler vanished, Mussolini was shot. Peace was signed and I was told at Radley that I shouldn't be wanted any more after the Service members of the staff came back from the war.

"At the end of July we went back to Porthcawl, where Jill found sleep and regained her strength and poise.

"On the day that Japan surrendered I was broadcasting in Birmingham. By Christmas all was well again. The war was over.

"I remember saying somewhere that that was the only completely successful Christmas of my life. I was well, I was getting up at three o'clock every morning and working like hell. I was broadcasting again and writing a good many articles. I had paid off my debts, I had been lecturing to a number of girls' and boys' schools, including Eton, Cheltenham, Tonbridge and Rossall, I was making money. I had finished my novel *Caper Sauce*.

The difficult thing is to convince oneself when the evil spirit is in possession that it will ever be exorcised. When I sit at my desk and can't find any words, when I misspell the simplest words and can't finish a sentence, it's difficult to have faith and believe that the tide will turn, the pen run over the page easily. What I can never foresee is when the tide will turn or what causes me to switch so quickly. It isn't always the arrival of a cheque.

"It's only during the last five years that I've had these alternate moods of despair and triumph. It's as difficult to account for these changes as it is to account for the chanciness of scent when we're out hunting, or the chanciness of one's form at cricket. It can't be just the state of my physical health because some of the best books have been written by men like R. L. Stevenson dying of consumption.

"One certain fact is that I only come alive in the sun. I missed desperately the chance of getting abroad during the war. Ever since it stopped I've seized every opportunity to get out of England and the result has been amazing.

"However ill I've felt, however dispirited, I've become a new man within a day of getting into the sun of the Alps or of the Riviera. Last Summer we went to Norway and I was as flat when I came back as I was when I started out.

"On the other hand I went out to Wengen at Christmas and within 24 hours I was right back in my top form.

"And even though she doesn't ski, Jill becomes herself again as she walks in the sun. She practically adopted the Scheidegg as her spiritual home at Christmas. She falls under the spell of the mountains, so long as they're in the sun, just as I do.

"The Oxford climate gets both of us down. It's hard to realize it when I'm on top of the world as I am now, but we spent the whole of every afternoon of last Summer term sitting in St. John's gardens, Jill knitting, I asleep, dozing or just watching the foreigners pass by. I no longer bathe in the Cherwell. The dirt and colour disgust me. I no longer ride in Port Meadows now that David Skeggs has gone."

"Who?"

"Oh! Of course you don't know. I'd better go on being chronological, so far as I can, without a diary to refer to. My memory very quickly becomes a blank.

"Where were we? Oh, January 1946. We went back as usual to Brighton. Lalage, Imogen and I found an unexploded mine on the beach. We followed the Crawley and Horsham foxhounds on foot over the Weald and over the Downs.

"I attended, as President, the first cricket supper for seven years at Southwick and got Gillie Potter, Maurice Tate and Arthur Gilligan to come as my guests. I invited Laidman Browne, who couldn't come, but sent in his place a most moving poem to explain his absence. Shall I recite it to you?"

"Do."

I did. Here it is:

"The moment I read your kind invitation
To join with the cricketers in celebration,
I rushed up the stairs to a box in the attic
Where, wrapped up in parcels with herbs aromatic,
Lay white socks, white shoes, white shirts and white pants
Protected, I hoped, from the moths and the ants.
Away flew the mothballs, away flew the dust,
For the place is a harbour for cobwebs and rust;
And there, in their glory, resplendent and fine,
'The raiment of Princes,' I cried, 'and all mine!'
I seized a broomhandle to use for a bat
And threw for a ball a crumpled old hat;
A swing and a swipe, and I hit it for six—
Since when I've been creeping about on two sticks.
The tang of the leather, the click of the bail,
The chase to the bound'ry, the quick pint of ale,
While the roller's pushed out for a bump on the wicket;
And a man is at peace—It is life—It is cricket.
So now, in reply to your warm friendly letter,
Let me say at the start how much I'm your debtor.
But I have to go North on the seventh of Jan.;
A duty a fellow must do if he can.
For the home team is losing a mighty long match,
The Field's round the wicket, all set for a catch,
And the grimmest of bowlers has taken the ball
While my Mother takes guard for her last game of all.
She has carried her bat, and for her reward
Already she's got eighty-two on the board.
But the old arms are tired, her guard's not so grand,
And we can do nothing but pray in the stand.
Forgive, then, my absence from Southwick this day,
Some future occasion, perhaps, if I may?
I have written in rhyme, and I've written in jingle,
With one or two hair-raising snicks for a single.
But on the great day that your wicket is pitched
I'll find myself far away, snookered, and bitched.
                           LAIDMAN BROWNE."

"You do have the nicest friends," said Penelope.

"I've promised my ghost that it shall spend its days hovering above Southwick Green. After all, I saved it for the village.

"In February I took Jill and Priscilla up to Fortingall."

"Fortingall? Where's that?"

"It's in Perthshire, in Glen Lyon. Jill and I are always escaping there. I first went there when I was an undergraduate with Douglas McNair. Then after the First World War a friend of mine, a Yorkshireman from Pontefract, called Bill Heptinstall, took over the small hotel there and made an international name for himself. He had learnt how to cook in Paris, he was a friend of André Simon and a member of the Wine and Food Society. You wouldn't expect to find Polish and Viennese dishes in a hamlet in the Highlands, but he produced the most unexpected exotic dishes. On Sunday mornings he had a cold table before luncheon containing over seventy different varieties of *hors-d'œuvres*.

"We went to Perth Bull Show and saw a Shorthorn bull, Pitoodrie Upright, sold for 14,500 guineas.

"I bought my usual suit in Aberfeldy, where I have bought all my suits for over twenty years.

"On my return to Oxford I did a quite mad thing. I bought a tiny house on the top of St. Giles' Hill, Winchester, for £4,000. I wanted a hill, dry soil, and sun. But as soon as I had paid for it, or rather as soon as the bank had paid for it, I panicked and tried to resell it. After nearly going out of my mind with anxiety I sold it at a slight loss and breathed again.

"It taught me a lesson. I shan't try to leave Oxford again. I shall die in this semi-detached villa. I have never before lived in any house longer than four years. Already I've lived in this one for over ten years and the rent is £100 a year. We spent our Summer holidays in Ilfracombe again. We had been for so many years to Woolacombe that I couldn't think of anywhere else. It rained every day for seven weeks.

"That September we sent Imogen as a boarder to the Dragon, but we took her away when she was ten and a half and sent her to Cheltenham, where she was happy from the word 'Go'. She loved being in the same House as Lalage.

"And now I'm in a quandary. I've got no diary to consult. The only thing I've got to refresh my memory is my ledger. I see that we sold all our spare furniture in August 1946. We only got £123. I wrote a Sports Guide to Brighton for 100 guineas and I met topographical, though Hutchinsons have spurred me on to write a thriller once a year. I've not had as much success with these as I deserved; because they were eminently filmable, but the film people wouldn't look at them.

"I started going abroad again at Easter 1947. Johnson gave me £100 in advance of royalties to pay for the trip to Switzerland and I wrote up my diary each night of our stay.

"We started at Montreux and spent a golden month drinking *campari*, exploring shops, taking excursions on the Lake of Geneva and up the Rhône Valley. I had the bright idea of making Jill and Imogen also keep diaries and I cashed in on my family heavily.

"That Summer we made our headquarters in Tenby for my book *I Return to Wales*, and out of that trip I got two books by writing a second one on *Little England Beyond Wales*. I fell in love at sight with Tenby because of its age, its dignity, and the glory of its sands. We explored all the Edwardian castles and met R. M. Lockley, who then farmed in an island called Dinas close to Cardigan. We were taken round the county by Major Lloyd George, whose son was in my form.

"The following Spring (1948) we went back to Llanwrtyd to get more material for *I Return to Wales*, and when the children had gone back to school Jill and I took a car round North Wales.

The next Summer we spent in Ireland, where Imogen got pneumonia, but one incident in that visit stands out in my mind.

"At Christ Church in the rooms above mine lived an undergraduate called R. C. Barton, who told me of the wrongs done to Ireland by England.

"After the war the Black and Tans raided Barton's house and seeing the pennons of the 17th Lancers came to the conclusion that he had stolen them. He had to explain that his grandfather was Colonel of the regiment.

" 'I liked your English prisons,' he said quietly. 'I had four years of them.'

"He was one of the signatories of the Peace Treaty.

"As we got a short-sighted view of Ireland from our visit to Bray, where we made our headquarters, Jill and I went back later in the year and stayed at Waterville, Co. Kerry, and Clifden, Connemara. The west of Ireland is about as good as the east is bad. This is one of those instances where the presence or absence of the sun made no difference. At Bray the sun shone all and every day and we disliked it. In the west of Ireland we never saw the sun. It rained all and every day, and we loved it.

"At Christmas we returned again to Switzerland, not to write about it but to enjoy the ski-ing at Villars. If there is a finer view in the world than that from Villars across the Rhône Valley to the Dent du Midi, I wish you'd tell me where it is. I spent all my days on the ski-slopes with Lalage and Imogen and all my nights dancing in the hotel. It was one of the most perfect holidays of my life.

"We spent Easter 1949 in Stratford-upon-Avon, collecting material for my book *Arden and Avon*. I was so ill that I couldn't even talk to A. L. Rowse and Alan Herbert, who came down as guests of honour to the Birthday Luncheon. I wrote my book and had to tear it up. I went back in October and saw an entirely different Stratford.

"Owing mainly to the generosity of Christopher Rookes, the owner of the Falcon Hotel, I was fêted and given a royal time. Everything fell into my lap. We were asked to all the big houses, and in one of them, Coughton Court, Jill discovered the portrait of Sir Charles Throckmorton (1757–1840), who was the image of me. I discovered that Warwickshire is fuller of great houses that still remain in the possession of the original owners than any other county.

"Mr. Ferrers of Baddesley Clinton, on discovering that I was a Petre, gave me a fine engraving of a Lord Petre of the eighteenth century.

"We were entertained to luncheon by Lord Bearsted at Sunrising, above Edgehill.

"We were given a Lucullan banquet by Tommy Bouch of Ashorne. He had been Master of the Belvoir when I was at Cranwell and I had made friends with him then. In addition to being a great sportsman he is a poet and an art connoisseur. We also went to see my friend Air Commodore Verney of Lighthorne, who had also been at Cranwell with me.

"I discovered a lot about Warwickshire, notably about Guy Fawkes and Ann Whatley of Temple Grafton, to whom Shakespeare would undoubtedly have been married had not Ann Hathaway's people forced him to marry the wrong Ann. I wrote a good book about that.

"That Summer we went to the Riviera for the first time in my life. We stayed at Menton, which is cheaper than anywhere else because it has a shingle beach instead of sand. I liked it better than anywhere else except Juan-les-Pins. The sea was marvellously warm

I

# CHAPTER XII

## BROADCASTING: I AM FADED OUT (1937-49)

I LOOKED round to make sure that Penelope was present.

"The subject," I said, "is broadcasting in war-time.

"We were in Woolacombe when war broke out. The B.B.C., who had established new secret headquarters at Wood Norton, just outside Evesham, had offered me 50 guineas together with billeting accommodation for a four weeks' series of talks to schools. The journey there was memorable. A great friend of mine had gone crazy the night before I was due to go and his friends implored me to go with him in his car and drop him off at a private mental home in Gloucester. It was killing two birds with one stone. Jill and I would get a free passage and my friend would have our companionship for his last free (in another sense) drive. I sat up with him most of the night before we left. Among other suggestions that he put forward was a pilgrimage to Iona, buying up the Musical Festival at Malvern, buying a million eggs in Hatch Beauchamp, and, most interesting of all, a game at Lord's.

" 'The Gentlemen of England,' he said; 'we can get them together by Tuesday. You'll go in first wicket.'

"I told him, which was true, that I had never gone in first wicket for the Gentlemen at Lord's. 'It may be difficult to get a side together quickly,' I said. 'They'll most of them be joining their regiments. Don't forget there's a war on.'

" 'What nonsense!' he said. 'There's no war on. All this talk about war. There's no war.'

"He's as right as a trivet now. Madness, like everything else, passes. The journey worried Jill a great deal more than it worried me. It was an open car and she sat at the back plying him with pills when the fit came on. I sat in front with his chauffeur.

"We had a nasty moment at the toll-bridge over the Parrot because we had to fill up with petrol and he refused to buy Pool. 'I never buy anything but Shell,' he shouted. 'If you won't let me have Shell, we'll drive on without petrol.' He then demanded chocolate.

" 'It must be Meunier, nothing but Meunier.'

"We daren't, as you will understand, stop anywhere for a meal, and by the afternoon we were practically passing out for lack of food. At Tewkesbury he struck, and we had to stop at a café. He immediately offered the woman £5,000 for the business and she, terrified, threatened to send for the police. We bundled him back into the car with the chauffeur and watched him drive off to Gloucester.

"Our day's adventures had only just begun. We took a bus on to Evesham. On getting out in the High Street I asked the nearest policeman to direct me to the billeting office of the B.B.C.

"To my surprise he arrested me.

" 'There ain't no B.B.C. here,' he said. 'You're a spy.'

"He was very pleased with himself as he roughly presented me to the Superintendent.

" ' 'Ere's a bloke enquiring about the B.B.C.'

"The Superintendent was more polite.

" 'There's no B.B.C. here,' he said. 'Who told you that there was?'

" 'As I've got to go on the air straight away,' I replied, 'you might as well cut that out.'

"The Superintendent roared with laughter.

" 'Have I said anything funny?' I said, getting a bit rattled. I was very tired.

" 'My friend the constable has,' he replied, and turning to the policeman said, 'Don't you ever listen in?'

" ' 'Course I do,' said the constable.

"The Superintendent turned again to me. 'Go on talking,' he said.

"I went on talking till he stopped me.

" 'Well, if you don't recognize that voice,' said the Superintendent, 'you damned well ought to. It's the best-known voice in England. Don't you recognize S. P. B. when you hear him?'

" 'Who?' asked the constable.

" 'S. P. B.,' repeated the Superintendent.

" 'M, A, I, S,' I said. 'S for Sugar.' "

Penelope laughed.

"You made that bit up."

"Jill was there. Ask her."

"Go on."

"The streets were full of young B.B.C. women in trousers and young B.B.C. producers in beards. They looked odd in this market-town. The billeting officer gave me an address and when we got to the door of the house the woman who opened it seemed surprised.

" 'The B.B.C. tell me,' I said, 'that you have a room reserved for me.'

" 'I've only one spare room,' she said, 'and that's occupied by my daughter.'

" 'She'll have a surprise,' I said, 'when she discovers that she's sharing it with me.'

"The woman slammed the door in my face.

"Eventually we were despatched to an old manor house and this time we were given sanctuary in a servant's bedroom in an attic. This is where Jill broke down. There were spiders and there were rats, and she's allergic to both."

"Poor Jill," said Penelope.

"Poor both of us," I said. "It was a strange start to war-time broadcasting. My first job was to go on the air and tell the evacuated townees on no account to eat the mushrooms that they found in the fields.

" 'All but one variety,' I said, 'are poisonous.'

"I got over a thousand letters pointing out all but one variety were edible. It was fun.

"The B.B.C. headquarters was hidden in a wood. You couldn't pass the golden gates at the bottom of the drive without giving the password. Bloodhounds patrolled the woods which were bounded by an electric fence. The recording vans were all camouflaged with the branches of trees. They looked like Birnam Wood on its way to Dunsinane. It hadn't occurred to them that it was Autumn and that leaves fall.

"It was an unreal life. James McKechnie—or was it Valentine Dyall?—lived in a caravan in a field on the banks of the Avon just outside the gates. We used to bathe there.

"I went back after the war on one hot summer Sunday afternoon with Lalage and Imogen from Cheltenham in order to let them bathe.

"The only other occupants of the water were two German prisoners of war now working on the land. The whirligig of time!

" 'Hogsnorton', as we called it, was a curious set-up.

"I had one glorious comeback as the result of my 'Edible Fungi' talk. It was a postcard and ran:

Go back to your village green and keep your mouth shut. Don't you know there's a war on?

"'That was the first time that I had heard that phrase.

"In point of fact (this was the 'phoney war' period) nobody knew there was a war on, though we nightly expected to be bombed out.

"Hitler had us pinpointed all right, but he was waiting. Heaven knows what for. I took to journeying to Evesham to broadcast and back to Exmoor to teach. I went on applying for a job. Almost all my high-up friends in the Ministries found time to reply. All of them repeated that I was much too valuable not to be used in some important capacity.

"'The only 'important capacity' that materialized was an invitation to go to Liverpool and censor German letters. As I hadn't a word of German or of French that was about the only job that I could not tackle, but practically everybody else in the country could. I didn't accept that invitation. I can't remember much about that fantastic time. It was all far away and long ago. I remember that one of my women chiefs was refused a billet because she wasn't an expectant mother. I remember that three hundred actors and actresses in London wrote to the B.B.C. asking for work. We had the Repertory Company, of course. We had the Variety Band. We had everybody. We were the funniest mixture of grave and gay, foreigners, infidels, heretics and Turks. We were proper maids-of-all-work. I remember giving a talk on Joan of Arc. I remember encountering Moray McLaren in the woods dressed up as captain of the night guard. I remember a porter at Taunton Station who saw the initials S. P. B. M. on my attaché-case and said:

"'The one and only.'

"'Yes,' I said. 'Mais, M, A, I, S. S for Sugar.'

"A man in the cloakroom at Exeter on the same day also spied my attaché-case and used precisely the same expression.

"'The one and only S. P. B. M.'

"It's funny to think that I was as well known as that once. It was only eleven years ago. It made me feel like a million dollars. Today I feel like a ha'penny dropped in a crowded street that no one even sees, and if they did wouldn't trouble to pick up.

"I gave talks on roads, caterpillars, diaries, fields, Tom Sawyer, nuts——"

"Nuts?"

"Nuts. A mixed bag. I was then transferred from Evesham to Bristol, and when the bombing began we got our fair share.

"Then the Midland Regional people sent me out with David

Gretton on a new sort of venture. It was called 'The Microphone At Large'.

"I first made a name for myself on the air just twenty years ago with a series called 'This Unknown Island', in which I selected seventeen places haphazard, and took about a week exploring each place and meeting people. I went to Haworth, Glastonbury, Cornwall, Galloway, North Wales, Norfolk, the Fens and the Peak. No one knew where I was going to next. I had been writing books about England for about eleven years before this, but my sales were negligible. Now by talking about these places instead of writing about them I had become a public figure. I was as well known then as Wilfred Pickles is now. On the whole my correspondents were enthusiastic. I remember one writer who said that I had the soul of a poet, the mind of a scholar and the character of a gentleman. To offset that an anonymous well-wisher described me as a talking potato. 'Get back,' he said, 'to your unfortunate village and on the green there spout to your damned silly self till the cows come home.' I annoyed the teetotallers by telling them how much I enjoyed my whiskey or beer at the end of the day, and hundreds of people wrote in to the B.B.C. asserting that I was being subsidized by the distillers and brewers. It was astonishing suddenly to find myself a best-seller. I've never recovered. So I was pleased when they put me on to 'The Microphone At Large'. There was, however, one big difference between this programme and 'This Unknown Island'. In the island talks I was alone. In the 'Microphone' talks I was interviewing country people and encouraging them to talk about their work. Before the war I had had a good deal of success televising craftsmen."

"I'd no idea that you televised as well."

"Blacksmiths, tattooists, potters, weavers, basket-makers and so on. It was fun. Just broadcasting them wasn't half such fun. My job was to put them at their ease. I was a bit too eager to talk myself. They told me I was too didactic. 'Come along, boy, come along, speak up.' You know the sort of thing. Wilfred Pickles has the supreme gift of making his interviewers feel on top of the world. I suppose I bullied mine. I didn't mean to, but people said that I frightened them, made them tongue-tied. That, of course, if it was true, was fatal. That's the reason they banished me from 'Country Magazine'. It was on the same lines as 'The Microphone At Large' except that in 'Country Magazine' the country had to come to town, and in 'The Microphone' the town went to the country. You see

1. PETRE, IMOGEN AND JILL ON THE EGGLI. 2. IMOGEN AT WENGEN, CHRISTMAS 1950. 3. PETRE AND JILL AT THE PALACE ICE BAR, WENGEN. 4. PETRE TEACHING IMOGEN TO SKI AT WENGEN. 5. JILL AT GSTAAD, 1951. 6. PETRE AND IMOGEN AT WENGEN SKI-JUMPS.

JILL

LALAGE

IMOGEN

AN ANCESTOR?

PETRE

where I went wrong. I was used to having the microphone to myself for an uninterrupted twenty minutes. I resented these people, almost inarticulate. I thought that I ought to be their interpreter. I resented far more the thing known as effects. You've only to mention the word 'sea' on the air and immediately the air is filled with the cries of seagulls. I'm going to write a novel some day called *Nobody Ordered Seagulls*. You've read *Nobody Ordered Wolves*? No? It's a satiric attack on the films by Jeffrey Dell. I want to debunk the B.B.C. in the same way. Look out for *Nobody Ordered Seagulls*."

"It's a grand title."

"And it's my copyright. Remember that."

"I'll remember. Go on."

"Where was I? Oh! 'The Microphone At Large'. I was getting uppish, too big for my boots. I made the mistake of thinking that I was indispensable. I accepted the fact that I was an ace broadcaster, a golden voice. Queer, because I'm essentially modest."

"I'll say you're modest. You've got a funny idea of yourself. Modest? All right. Go on."

"I'll tell you when I wasn't modest. I did a talk in the series 'I Was There'. I imagined myself a schoolboy in Derby on the Black Friday when Prince Charles Edward turned back. It was so good that listeners really thought they were back in 1745 and that they were listening to a Derby Grammar School boy of that year. That was my finest hour!"

"You were talking about 'The Microphone At Large'."

"Was I? Thanks for the memory. I wish you could have heard 'I Was There'."

"I'm here. Isn't that enough for you?"

"My darling listener."

"Yes, I suppose all listeners are darling."

"They're my meat and drink."

"Commercial, aren't you?"

"What was I talking about?"

"Still at large with the microphone."

"I suppose that really is the secret of it."

"Secret of what?"

"The B.B.C.'s cold shoulder. I don't like features. I like things straight. All this breaking up with music and noises off. It's like the cheap Press breaking up the news. All right for half-wits. I can read. Give me *The Times*. I can listen. Give me a straight talk. The B.B.C.

have pandered and kow-towed to an imaginary audience that demands dialect, the common voice, and features."

"You ought to have been Lord Reith."

"I got on with him like a house on fire. I've always liked my chiefs. Freddie Ogilvie was a grand chap. I remember once when the bombs were falling as quickly as the rest of Europe I was doing my funny stuff on the 'Kitchen Front', following the news. I got a telephone message from Freddie. 'Terrific,' he said. 'Come to breakfast.'

"I went across Portland Place to breakfast and the first thing he said was, 'I think you know my wife.'

"I was a bit tired, what with bombs and being funny about food. I disclaimed all knowledge of her.

"Lady Ogilvie appeared, smiling, in the doorway.

"She said: 'You've forgotten. We've met before. I was an undergraduate at Cambridge, so was my friend. We were too scholars going back after the Christmas vac from Scotland. We were alone in the carriage. Suddenly the door opened and a hatless man, all wrapped up in scarves and several greatcoats, rushed in and said, "You two look cold and hungry—come and have some food." You took us to the dining-car and fed us. Bless you. Do you always act the knight-errant to lonely females in distress?' "

"Do you?" asked Penelope.

"Invariably. What was I talking about?"

" 'The Microphone At Large'. You know, I don't think we're going to get far with that. We've had too many false starts. Tell me about television."

"Ally Pally," I began.

"Ally Pally?" echoed Penelope.

"Our term of endearment for the Alexandra Palace, so called because it's not in an alley but on the top of a high hill, and not pally, but the most intimidating ugly great barracks of a place I was ever in. Furthermore it's the most inaccessible place near London. It's easier to take the night train to Edinburgh than it is to get to Ally Pally. We had to have a special bus which wound its way through the dreariest, meanest streets that even London can boast. If you want the quickest way to feeling suicidal try going from Portland Place to Ally Pally. It's unbelievable. Such dreary people, such infernos of slums. When after hours and hours you actually reach it you think you've been transported to the South Shore, Blackpool. It's full of the sort of sordid amusements that you think of when you say 'Fun Fair'. It means an interminable dreary walk over ground which is rich in litter, otherwise completely barren. Except for a few slot-machines the Palace itself is the sort of Palace that Minos, King of Crete, built for his Minotaur, all labyrinth.

"First there was the make-up room."

"Make-up room? It's not a theatre."

"That's just what it is. To me the words are a little indecorous. I only know it of course from the films, where girls who are all legs and scanties sit in front of mirrors and start taking their stockings off or putting them on.

"A most attractive girl started doing something to my eyebrows."

"That must have been nice for you."

"It would have been if I could have seen her. I had to keep my eyes shut. She then did something to my lily-white hands."

"You must have changed a lot."

"I haven't changed at all."

"Look at your hands."

"That's bringing the coal in. When she'd finished bleaching and whitening me I looked at myself in the glass. It may have been a face. It wasn't my face. I looked like a man who had borne all the sorrows of the world on his shoulders and was about to be hanged for a crime that he hadn't committed. Luckily I was given no time to think. I was hustled across the passage into a vast studio where I was blinded by arclights under which I sweated, partly with the terrific heat and partly with fear. There were cameramen posted on cameras on wheels who darted at me like snakes, there were bevies of luscious young things in *décolletée* evening gowns."

"They ought to have put you at your ease."

"They helped. One of them, a dazzling creature, came up smiling and said that she was my announcer.

" 'That's better,' she said. 'So you can smile.'

" 'Hold my hand,' I said. She did. I began to think that television had something when I suddenly recollected that I had no script.

"The only reason that I didn't become an actor (I've a passion for the stage) is that I can't remember my lines. I love acting."

"So I've noticed," said Penelope. "You're putting on an act most of the time."

"It's in my blood. As I was saying, I can't remember lines. So I really was frightened on being brought into the limelight and then told to hold myself up and be natural. Being photographed is a frightful ordeal for me. I'd far rather have a tooth drilled."

"Yes, you give that impression in all the photographs I've ever seen of you."

"In television I was not only being photographed. I was expected to talk rationally and entertainingly at the same time. I was describing sheep-shearing on the South Downs. It was hell. It was worse than doing a running commentary on the sound-track while you're looking at the film of the thing you're talking about."

"Yet you liked it."

"I liked my craftsmen series, because watching skilled men at work is always fun, and if you dry up the viewer can still be looking at the bodger or the potter, or whatever he is. I liked enormously the punch party that Arthur Street gave."

"What was the idea of that?"

"Conviviality and good conversation over the punchbowl, to give the viewers a chance of seeing their favourite broadcasters letting their hair down. I forget what we talked about. We drank a lot. It was a roaring success."

"You weren't frightened?"

"If he's had enough to drink, no man is frightened. I wonder sometimes . . ."

"You wonder what?"

"Whether I shouldn't still be broadcasting if I'd had enough to drink. You see, in the 'Country Magazine' programme I got on all right with the farmers, and so on, whom I had to compère, but we only had one pint of beer between the run-through and the show itself, and I wanted gin."

"But surely you're not a farmer?"

"I come from farming stock. I know the difference between barley and oats. I agree that I don't know so much about it as Arthur Street or Ralph Wightman, but we never had a flop when I had the job. I've staged a come-back at everything else—books, teaching, dramatic criticisms, book-reviewing, and so on, but not the B.B.C."

"You've written to them?"

"I've done nothing but."

"You've been to see them?"

"I'm not the sort of chap to prop up a bar on the offchance of running into a programme director."

"That's the way to get a job in Fleet Street!"

"How do you know?"

"You say so in one of your books. 'Never write a letter, always call at the office.' "

"Did I say that?"

"You did."

"Then, as Wilfred Pickles would say, I was dead right."

"Let's get back to 'The Microphone At Large'."

"Oh, yes. We took the van to Rockingham because it's still feudal and under the suzerainty of the Culme-Seymours. It forms an exciting contrast to Corby just up the hill, which is all bulldozers and belching smoke from the foundries. Then we went to the Wyre Forest to talk to the timber-fellers. Then to Stow-on-the-Wold to have a look at the quarries, then to Uttoxeter to make sure that the heart of England was still beating, then to Weobley to see some witches and black-and-white houses, then to Southam. It was an interesting experience. In the 'Unknown Island' series I tried to make listeners see the places. In 'The Microphone At Large' listeners heard the authentic voices of the people. It was a sounder interpretation of England."

"What did your fans think about it? I suppose you got thousands of letters?"

"Thousands. I always did. Some of the criticism was constructive. One correspondent complained that the microphone wasn't at large. It was pinned to one central spot. Somebody else complained that he was conscious all the time of a group of people sitting round the room, all self-conscious and very much afraid of the microphone. I agree that it would have been better to have interviewed farmers in their own farmyards. We did that in 'Rural Rides' in the Cobbett country. It went down well."

"Did they tell you what they liked best?"

"Most people wrote to complain, of course. But nearly everybody wrote in to say how delighted they were to hear the old clock on the mantelpiece in the Wyre Forest strike eight when it was really five minutes past."

"So much for 'The Microphone At Large'. What then?"

"I kept on broadcasting to schools until my chief told me that my voice had become too dictatorial or inaudible, I forget which. I've never talked down to children, and I've never been inaudible in my life.

"The best talk I ever gave in my life was in 'I Was There', when I pretended to be a boy in Derby in 1745. I've told you about that. I did it in dialect. The B.B.C.'s got a thing about dialect. Then I did a talk on China Clay, a glorious feature programme on 'Sussex by the Sea', and some Sunday Night Appeals."

"Oh! You were as popular as all that?"

"Then one on Lundy, a lovely feature, one on Burford, almost as exciting, one on the Mendips—and then came the war . . . and I was blacked out."

"You went to Evesham."

"The beginning of the end. Evesham was all right. Bristol was all right. Birmingham was all right, London was all right except for the bombs. I was doing something to help win the war when they put me on to talk to America every week. They were good talks. And there was Manchester. I was on the Overseas Service, the Home Service, the Scottish Regional, the South African Service, the American network, the North Regional, the Midland Regional, the West Regional."

"This doesn't sound like fading out."

"For one week I did a nightly turn at the Trocadero, I got thirty quid for telling Londoners that the smell of horse manure was better than the smell of tarmac and petrol. I might as well have been talking Greek, so I told them how near I came to being King of Albania. They understood that and cheered me to the echo.

"I miss my broadcasting more than I can say. I was a good broadcaster. Everybody said so, and now wherever I go I have to listen to the same remark: 'We don't seem to have heard you on the air lately, Mr. Mais. Why?' "

I was expecting some answer to that, or some consolation, perhaps a touch of that delicate hand on my hair, but no. Penelope made no comment.

I turned round petulantly.

She wasn't there.

# CHAPTER XIII

## I Come Back to Books (1940–51)

PENELOPE (I had forgotten her existence) said from the depths of the bookshelves:

"You've written a lot of books. How many?"

I turned round to see her lying on her stomach reaching out for books on the lowest shelf, where I keep my own works.

"Too many. Far too many. I've lost count. Call it a hundred and fifty."

"You ought to be pleased."

"On the contrary. I'm ashamed of most of them."

"Don't tell me that you don't get a thrill each time the parcel of author's copies arrives."

"There's no hiding anything from your devastating eye. I do. It doesn't last."

"You're too modest."

"No. The royalty sheets prove how right I am. The public and I are of the same mind. I'm not a best-seller."

"Some of them must have had big sales."

"*The English Course for Schools* and *This Unknown Island*. That's all."

"How many did they sell?"

"About 20,000 each."

"What about the novels?"

"You'll have to ask Hutchinsons."

"But some of them are really exciting."

"I wish the film people thought so. I seem to miss the boat each time."

"How long does it take you to write a book?"

"A little longer than Edgar Wallace. A good deal less time than Edward Gibbon. When I get an idea I rush at it. I'm terribly careless, but I work like mad when the first fine careless rapture is on me. I get up long before dawn every morning and chuck all the work I ought to be doing, become unbearable in the house, am frightfully pleased with myself for half a dozen chapters, then I leave it to do something else, and usually forget about it for ever. I'm a poor sort of writer."

"What are you on now?"

"I've got no fewer than fourteen books on the stocks, and I flit from one to the other, just as I flit about from chapter to chapter in my novels. I never write straight ahead."

"It sounds needlessly complicated."

"That's the way I write. I can't help it."

"Where do you get your inspiration?"

"From God, from the countryside, from travelling, from chance meetings with people like you."

"How many books have you written since 1937?"

"When I was broadcasting I didn't write any. Now that I'm no longer broadcasting I do nothing else. One must express oneself somehow. After all—oh, hell!"

Penelope looked up from the bookshelf.

"Why the 'Oh, hell!'?"

"You're too young to remember what *Punch* said about *Interlude* —my first novel."

"Tell me."

"Willingly. Listen:

" 'Mr. Mais has given us a piece of character drawing almost flawlessly perfect. Not for a very long time has it been my good fortune to attend such a triumph, and I wish to proclaim it. I feel sure that he has within him the qualities that go to make a great novelist, and that his future lies straight and clear before him.'

"It was worth while being sacked from schoolmastering to get a notice like that. But what happened? *Punch* hasn't even deigned to notice any book of mine or say one word either in praise or dis-praise since that date. I was a great man once, a great novelist, a great schoolmaster, a great broadcaster. What came over me? It can't just be age. I'm young for sixty-six."

"I'll say you're young. You're talking like a petulant child of six. Nobody can do better than his best."

"Oh, Penelope, that's unworthy of you! No *clichés*, please, or I shall cry."

"All right. Go on talking. So you're a failure, you can't write a novel, you can't teach, you can't broadcast. In other words, you've had it?"

"No, I haven't had it. I'll write a good book yet."

"Of course you will. In the meantime it might restore your self-esteem if you gave me a list of all the books you have written since 1937."

"I shall have to look them up in *Who's Who*!"

"What's wrong with that? It's a sign of greatness to forget the past."

I looked up *Who's Who* and groaned.

"Now what's the matter?"

"I couldn't believe that I had written so much that I had forgotten."

"Read out the list."

I read out the list.

| | | | |
|---|---|---|---|
| The Three-coloured Pencil | 1937 | I Return to Switzerland | 1948 |
| Let's Get Out Here | 1937 | I Return to Ireland | 1948 |
| Light Over Lundy | 1938 | Who Dies? | 1948 |
| Old King Coal | 1938 | The Land of the Cinque Ports | 1948 |
| Walking in Somerset | 1938 | Little England Beyond Wales | 1948 |
| Britain Calling | 1938 | I Loved You Once | 1948 |
| Highways and Byways in the | | The English Scene Today | 1948 |
| Welsh Marches | 1939 | Southern Rambles | 1949 |
| Listen to the Country | 1939 | The Best in Their Kind | 1949 |
| Hills of the South | 1939 | The Riviera: New Look and | |
| Fifty Years of the L.C.C. | 1939 | Old | 1950 |
| Raven Among the Rooks | 1939 | We Wander in the West | 1950 |
| The Man in Blue Glasses | 1940 | Winter Walks in Kent | 1950 |
| There'll Always Be An Eng- | | Winter Walks in Surrey | 1950 |
| land | 1940 | Madeira Holiday | 1951 |
| A Cluster of Grapes | 1941 | Arden and Avon | 1951 |
| Diary of a Citizen in War- | | Britannia 1651–1951 | 1951 |
| time | 1941 | The Story of Oxford | 1951 |
| The Black Spider | 1941 | Winter Sports Holiday | 1951 |
| Youth After the War | 1943 | Norwegian Odyssey | 1951 |
| Caper Sauce | 1947 | Austrian Holiday | 1951 |
| I Return to Scotland | 1947 | Come Love, Come Death | 1951 |
| I Return to Wales | 1948 | | |

"and *Buffets and Rewards*, 1952."

"In preparation, as they say: *Thy Protestant, Europa, Mediterranean Holiday, Buffets and Rewards*. Well?"

"Give me time to get my breath back. . . ."

"As long as you like."

The pause wasn't as long as I expected.

"So you're an old 'ham', the forgotten man, the man who couldn't stage a come-back. Well, well."

She paused again.

"Is that all?" I said.

K

"No. It's not all. I know what you're waiting for. You're waiting for me to give you a clap on the back. 'At any rate you've not sat down under it', and all that. I suppose you realize that you've crammed the whole lifetime of many less energetic authors into a mere thirteen years, of which six were spent in the worst war of all time?"

"If only they were better books."

"Well, out of—how many is it?—over forty, some of them must have given pleasure to someone. Tell me about those that displease you least."

"The kids' thrillers were all right," I said. "*Light Over Lundy*, *Raven Among the Rooks*, *The Three-coloured Pencil*, *The Man in Blue Glasses* and *The Black Spider* were good in their way. *Caper Sauce* was originally a good book. Bitter but true. I had to castrate that!

"I've only written three novels since then. *Who Dies?*, *I Loved You Once* and *Come Love, Come Death*."

"What about the non-fiction?"

"Machine-made, most of it. I should have been properly in the cart had it not been for the Southern Railway. It's fun going for walks in Kent and Surrey and being paid for it."

"Is that more paying than books?"

"Of course it is. It means £500 every time I do a booklet for the railway. Money for jam."

"Do they sell?"

"In millions."

"Why?"

"Because ramblers are lazy. They like the minimum of effort. They like to be told exactly where to turn right, where to stop for tea, what time to start, what time to stop."

"You don't describe the scene?"

"I don't wax lyrical."

"Most of your books are topographical."

"Nearly all. There were two anthologies. *A Cluster of Grapes* was cut in half because we couldn't pay the copyright fees of poets still alive. *The Best in Their Kind* was a good book, but escaped notice."

"What about all those 'Return' books?"

"They were fun to do. I had a publisher who knew something of the art of production. They sold like hot cakes to start with. Then when I'd got going the public had no more money for books. That's always my fate. I produced a book on the day of the General Strike in May 1926. It was killed stone dead."

"You seem to have been abroad a lot lately."

"Well, during the war we couldn't move, and I got a bad dose of claustrophobia. I have to go away every three months or so."

"How lucky to be able to."

"The publisher advances me a good deal in advance of royalties and the foreign transport authorities and hotels are usually forthcoming. After all, it's pretty useful publicity."

"I can see that. You aren't wholly without intelligence. If only you knew how to handle money you wouldn't always be on the verge of bankruptcy. Tell me about this *Britannia 1651–1951*. That sounds good."

"It's a new idea of mine. You know my passion for maps."

"I've only to look round the walls of this room."

"Well, I bought a complete atlas of Jansson 1651, and got Staples to reproduce the maps of all the English counties. I then wrote about 1,500 words of descriptive matter to sum up the spirit and achievement of each county to go on the appropriate page opposite each map."

"That's a really ingenious idea. I look forward to seeing it. That ought to be a winner anyway."

"They're always going to be winners. They never are."

"Have you kept a tally, as Trollope did, to show how much money you've got out of each book?"

"I haven't had time."

"I didn't think you had. Never mind."

# CHAPTER XIV

## WHO WOULD BE AN AUTHOR? (1951)

"You certainly look cute," said Penelope. "What's happened?"

"The lights have fused."

"Why are you whispering?"

"My voice has gone. I've got laryngitis. The first time in my life."

"It must be the first time this house has ever been quiet while you've been in it."

"As a matter of fact, I like it. Everybody speaks to me carefully and very loudly. They all think I'm deaf."

"Yes, but you mustn't strain your voice talking to me. I can hear your whispers as clearly as your ordinary voice. I like the silver candlesticks and the eight red candles."

"Seven. One's not working. Seven's my lucky number."

"It's very restful. This and the firelight. What are you poring over?"

"My royalties, sales and all that."

"That must make you feel proud."

"I don't know. On the same day that I got a letter from Sheffield asking where the writer could procure copies of all my works I was rung up by an unknown who asked me if I would accept copies of all my works. 'I am taking up psychology,' he said. 'I shan't have any use for them any more.' I agreed.

"Here's a list of the sales of all my early books and the royalties I got. These were published by the Richards Press. It only takes us up to 1936."

"Let's have a look."

I handed the list over. Here it is:

| TITLES | COPIES SOLD | £ |
|---|---|---|
| *From Shakespeare to O. Henry* | 3929 | 62 |
| *Books and Their Writers* | 2392 | 75 |
| *English Course for Schools* | 21109 | 472 |
| *Rebellion* | 1514 | 38 |
| *Lovers of Silver* | 1936 | 56 |
| *Education of a Philanderer* | 5449 | 75 |

| TITLES | COPIES SOLD | £ |
|---|---|---|
| Uncle Lionel | 2515 | 86 |
| Schoolmaster's Diary | 2854 | 75 |
| Colour Blind | 2608 | 119 |
| Breaking Covert | 2438 | 102 |
| Caged Birds | 2839 | 103 |
| Prunello | 3383 | 134 |
| Quest Sinister | 2847 | 106 |
| English Course for Everybody | 7982 | 218 |
| Oh, To Be in England | 2851 | 81 |
| Why We Should Read | 2299 | 79 |
| Orange Street | 6252 | 207 |
| Eclipse | 4517 | 169 |
| See England First | 10121 | 190 |
| Sussex | 2580 | 60 |
| It Isn't Far From London | 2765 | 77 |
| Perissa | 3737 | 134 |
| Some Books I Like | 2031 | 35 |
| Some Modern Authors | 2916 | 71 |
| High Lands of Britain | 2555 | 97 |
| Week-ends in England | 2741 | 103 |
| Round About England | 2201 | 150 |
| Shakespeare | 8600 | 20 |
| Dawn of British Literature | 4000 | 20 |
| More Books I Like | 696 | 12 |

"You don't seem to have made much out of your Shakespeare."

"You'll find this difficult to believe, but this is the first time I've even glanced at this list. You see, I loved Grant Richards, as did every other author who wrote for him, and in those halcyon days he published all the topnotchers. A. E. Housman, Masefield, everybody. He had a flair for discovering the best writers before anybody had even heard of them. He gave me my first chance. He gave Alec Waugh (who was a pupil of mine at Sherborne) his first chance. The contracts didn't seem to matter. When we wanted money we'd call at his office in Orange Street and he'd look down on us through his monocle and suggest luncheon at the Carlton Grill, a meal that he would always pay for by cheque, and by that time we forgot our mission, forgot everything except the good food, the good wine and the scintillating conversation. Grant Richards was one of the best friends I ever had. I used to stay with him in his lovely house at

Cookham Dean and also at his cottage at Poltesco in Cornwall. He always kept open house and I used to meet all the famous authors of the time in one or other of his homes. I also met Goya and Hélène, his daughters, both of whom were dazzling and, like him, affectionate.

"'Granty', as everyone called him, was far more a friend than a publisher. If was fun dunning him, and if he failed to stump up there was always luncheon at the Carlton. It was a joy to have him publish my books. I only wish that he were alive now. He'd have revelled in my autobiography. It's exactly his cup of tea."

"I'd like to compare these figures with some of the later ones."

"That's not going to be easy. Putnam sold over 20,000 of my first broadcast talks on 'This Unknown Island'.

"Hutchinsons have been my main publishers of late years. They printed 10,000 of my novel *Caper Sauce*. I was so afraid of libel, in spite of the fact that I'd deleted a comic scene at a private school to appease a friend, that I adopted a pseudonym, 'Michael Stone'. I had to pay £174 for alterations. It was already in page proof when I altered it."

"I don't remember any book by Michael Stone."

"No. In the end I decided to let it go under my own name. It wouldn't have sold half as many under a pseudonym, so the publishers said. But they sent in the royalties to Michael Stone."

"So you have got a faithful following, after all."

"Hutchinsons think so."

"Did they always print 10,000 of your novels?"

"No. They printed 6,500 of *I Loved You Once*. They seem to sell my novels. I noticed on the dust jacket of *Caper Sauce* that *The Black Spider* had sold 16,000."

"What sort of contracts do you get?"

"They vary a lot. What I usually try to bargain for is £200 payable in advance (on acceptance of the typescript) of a royalty of 15 per cent up to 5,000, and 20 per cent thereafter."

"But don't the agents fix all that?"

"I have had several agents. The snag about agents is that if they are top-line agents they have too many famous clients to worry over small fry, and if they are small agents the publishers don't look at their stuff. My Johnson sales and earnings up to 1951 were:

|  | Sales | Royalties |  |  |
|---|---|---|---|---|
|  |  | £ | s. | d. |
| I Return to Scotland | 9618 | 884 | 10 | 3 |
| I Return to Switzerland | 7129 | 708 | 7 | 0 |
| I Return to Ireland | 4852 | 511 | 0 | 1 |
| I Return to Wales | 3852 | 303 | 18 | 8 |
| The Land of the Cinque Ports | 3474 | 184 | 10 | 4 |
| Little England Beyond Wales | 3375 | 148 | 13 | 7 |
| The Riviera—New Look and Old | 2385 | 250 | 0 | 0 |
|  |  | £2990 | 19 | 11 |

"I've never made an outstanding success with any book yet, but I'm of Day Lewis's school of thought:

" 'If there is one thing which surpasses the ardour of concentration in writing a book it is the extreme sense of detachment I feel when it has been written. Every attempt is a wholly new start and a different kind of failure, so I cut myself free from each failure in order to make the next attempt.'

"I can't remember the plot or any of the characters of any novel that I have written. I am like a barrister who sweats his soul out to win the case for his client, but after the case is over erases the whole affair from his mind in order to be clear for his next case.

"I could wish that I wrote better. I'm always in a tearing hurry, always afraid lest I should die before the half-finished MS. is completed.

"All my works, except the broadcast talks, have a hurried atmosphere about them.

"But authorship, like bachelordom and spinsterhood, has its compensations. The arrival of an idea, the germination, the planning of the pattern, the pattern going according to plan, the finish (though that's as exhausting as the last lap of a three-mile race), and best of all the tearing open of the parcel that holds the author's six complimentary copies—all these are thrilling. I don't know why six copies of one's own work look so much more imposing than one.

"Then comes the search round the bookshops. My book seems never to be there. Everybody else is there, but not S. P. B. M. I feel completely deflated, and for weeks I can't think of anything to write. There was a brilliant fourth leader in *The Times* on this subject on 22nd June, 1951.

"I take billions of notes for each book, but I never refer to them. I used to think that the act of writing them down would keep them fresh in my mind, but it never does.

"My travel books are better because I take notes by day and write the book in the form of a diary from my notes every night. That is an ideal way of writing a book because when the holiday is over the book is written."

"But how can you find time if you're travelling all the time to write anything?"

"There's always an hour somewhere. While Jill and Imogen are dressing for dinner or between three in the morning and breakfast-time. Jill sits up in bed doing hers after breakfast. Both Jill and Imogen have a natural gift for writing.

"Imogen wrote a poem on Blindness which she sent to *Country Life*. She got a very encouraging letter back saying that Milton had written a similar one. 'Mine's better than his,' she said woefully."

"Is it?"

"I'll leave you to judge. Here it is:

"BLINDNESS
Now all is dark and everything so blank
    I do look back upon my days of light
When sky and sea and countryside I found
    So sweet and lovely to my wandering sight.

Yet, now I can imagine all that is,
    And yet I cannot see Thy wondrous earth.
I sometimes think of all my wasted life,
    And things that came before—my joy, my mirth.

O God, if Thou hast eyes enough to see,
    If Thou, O Lord, has heart enough to know,
Please let me see again Thy Kingdom upon earth
    Before Thou takest me away—before I go."

"Yes. I think she's right. What a child!"

"Yes, she's a flautist, clay-modeller, artist—she did wonderful dust jackets for *Who Dies?* and *Light Over Lundy*; she's a good mathematician, a Greek scholar, an omnivorous reader, outstandingly good at games, a House colour at cricket, tennis, hockey and lacrosse, and the best companion after Jill I've ever known. She's got everything—and now a poet. . . .

"Jill's something of a poet too. She wrote a poem for me to put on the title page of *Arden and Avon*, and the publisher forgot all about it."

"Can I hear that?"

"Of course. Listen:

> "I met a witch in Preston Street
> With lime-green coat and ermine tails;
> Minstrels, jugglers, charlatans, passers-by
> And sleety hailstones spiked her feet."

"She's got something there."

"Well, it makes me feel happier about dying. They'll both be able to make their living by writing. Jill wrote a pleasant article about me for *The Queen*, which was immediately accepted."

"Can I hear what she said about you? It ought to be fun."

"It is. Of course you shall hear it. Listen:

" 'How lucky you are; life for you is just one long holiday.'

This has been said to me so often and, indeed, compared with the lives of many of my friends, I feel it to be true.

Yet it is a way of life brought about by chance and a certain amount of planned work on my part, made possible since the children grew up (more or less, eighteen-thirteen), and the absence of staff.

Petre's work takes him all over the country during the Winter months for lectures, and I usually go with him.

Again, in the Summer months we take a long holiday which is always turned into a book, and again I go too, so that our lives are as much at ease when away as they are when at home.

Perhaps that is the kernel and key of our whole existence, this making light of travel and freedom at home.

Please don't run away with the idea that we have no home life. Between bouts of travel we settle down as Darby and Joan with a coal fire, dog and daughter and even do a certain amount of entertaining, and perhaps because of the extra effort of running our home alone and unaided, life to our friends appears, and on the whole becomes, just one long holiday.

However, I will confine my descriptions of Petre to holidays because at home, maybe through overwork, he is not always the best of companions.

Getting up at any hour ranging from 2.30 –4, working until breakfast and on until ten or eleven, when, if the weather be fine, he will go off to ride on Port Meadow, lunch at 'Vincent's', and then out with the Christ Church Beagles, so that I often don't see him until six, when he is quite naturally dropping with tiredness.

record that that is the only journey we have travelled on the same train separately.

Holidays for most people are usually spent in relaxation, but ours, as I said before, are a mixture of work and play.

Every journey we make, every place we visit, is all material for an author, and Petre, as well as taking thousands of notes on scraps of paper which he invariably loses, can read and understand time-tables, both bus and train.

Yes, for efficiency in getting to the ends of the earth I can thoroughly recommend Petre. Yet when we get there he becomes an unknown quantity, buying cigars, hats, maps, and, of course, books, all of which he has already packed from home, and refusing to buy what I call the essentials.

When we go a-roaming Petre always feels happier if he goes 'prepared'. This means that even though the day be fair at the start there is always the chance of a frost or sunstroke, at least in England, and he suspects earthquakes abroad.

So he sets out with shorts, a couple of waistcoats, socks and a pair of leggings, gym shoes and a pair of nailed boots, topped with a coat which is reversible, and a fishing hat, which, after all, is the same shape as a topee. Oh yes, and of course that gorgeous piece of red flannel he bought in Connemara which he uses as a scarf.

Then, of course, he has to have a bag for 'spares' just in case it rains. So I remember Petre, on that blazing day in San Remo, wearing shorts kept up with a white bathing belt, an O.U.A.C. blazer, a cap far back on his head, smoking a cigar which unpeeled like a cactus plant, carrying his thick reversible coat in one hand, and a zipper bag (little pig's bottom) packed with newly bought guide books and maps and my umbrella sticking out of one end, in the other, trying to write notes in all that heat and singing anything ribald that happened to enter his head.

On holiday, Petre usually manages to lose a hat, and the type bought is governed by the weather of that particular day.

This summer I had listened to and watched him admiring a white homburg-shaped summer hat worn by a fellow guest at the Hôtel de Paris in Menton, until one evening after dinner with the shops still open we wandered into a hat-shop. Here he became pernickety and womanlike, trying on about a dozen while Imogen and I pointed out the advantages or disadvantages of this and that particular shape and colour. Eventually he walked out of the shop unable to decide and told the patient assistant that he would return the next day when he could see the hats in sunlight.

Some days later we visited Juan-les-Pins and lurched into the first souvenir shop on the way to the sea. Here he found a smart light oatmeal chapeau for 590 fr. and got unexpectedly cross with me for not admiring and taking enough interest in this purchase, so bracing myself I praised it and him all the way to the sea.

For years on and off he has taken snuff, to my annoyance, because I wash his handkerchiefs, and I defy anyone to get snuffy white handkerchiefs clean however long they are boiled. On holiday this year he has, I notice, bought himself six delicious yellow silk handkerchiefs presumably with the idea that because they are yellow I shall not see the snuff stain.

Innocence, thy name is Petre, for does he really believe I can so easily be fooled? Silk mustn't be boiled anyway, and I've already pinched two to wear around my neck.

Yes, on holiday, exasperating he very often is, but boring never, and although I find myself frequently walking in the mud I also quite often see the stars."

—(Reprinted from *The Queen* by kind permission of the Editor.)

Penelope said nothing for about a minute.

"Well?" I said.

"She's obviously desperately in love with you and you hurt her. In point of fact the whole thing's a love-letter."

Suddenly she changed the subject.

"Who would be an author? You would."

"Anybody would who could call spirits from the vasty deep."

"So if you had your time over again you'd still choose to be an author?"

"I'd still choose to be an author, but I'd like to have been a better one. It would have been fun to see fellow-passengers in trains reading my books and liking them. It would have been thrilling to see my characters come to life in a film.

"The best I've done is to give a few thousand people some idea of where to spend their holidays and how to enjoy them. It's certainly been grand fun rediscovering Madeira, Norway, the Riviera, Switzerland, Ireland, Austria and the Mediterranean. Had I not written about them I should never have been able to travel, and I put travel very high up in the category of the things that make for man's happiness. In my case specially because I'm so dependent on the sun to make me merry and keep me well."

"It occurs to me," said Penelope, "that you ought, in your autobiography, to offer some sort of guidance to would-be authors who would be content to be even the sort of writer that you are."

"What can I tell them that can be of any use? That I find the best time of the day for writing is the five or six hours before breakfast? I only write that way because I can't sleep after three o'clock. Obviously it doesn't matter at all when you write so long as you do write. Most writers work at night and sit up. I'm usually in bed by ten o'clock and certainly my brain isn't functioning then. I write very fast and scratch out practically nothing. If you look at the MSS. of famous writers in the British Museum you'll find them all scrawled over with corrections.

"In my novels I don't wait to get the whole ground plan ready. I start off without the slightest idea where I am going.

"I write on the cheapest possible quarto sheets and I type nothing. Quite a number of authors type direct on to a machine; I need a pen in my hand. That is a pity because there are only two people in the world who can decipher my handwriting, Jill and Ethel Christian.

"I was asked a year or two ago by the A.O.C., H.Q. Bomber Command, to give a lecture in the camp and stay with him. I wrote back accepting and asking if I could bring my wife. I got a telegram in reply: *Delighted. Bring bitch but state size because of rationing.* I wrote back to say that my wife was not a bitch and that she weighed 9 st. 6 lb. and stood 5 ft. 7½ in. I got another telegram in reply to that which ran: *Some mistake surely. No bitch 9 st. 6 lb. We have two mastiffs. Better leave bitch behind.*

"I wrote the next letter in block capitals which elicited the reply: *By all means bring dog. Delighted.*

"When we arrived at the Air Marshal's house he greeted me with: 'I've put the mastiffs away. Where's this bitch you've got so fussed over?'

"'Here,' I said, introducing Jill. 'I wasn't fussing. It was she who insisted on coming.'

"'Heavens!' said the Air Marshal, 'and I've put you in a single bedroom!'

"'That's quite all right. She'll sleep with the mastiffs in the kennels.'

"It's quite a nuisance not being able to write legibly. In reply to my request for hotel tariffs in Austria, the tourist agency replied that they had no films in stock.

"In *I Return to Scotland* I didn't notice the fact that I let through the mis-statement that trams ran between Glasgow and Helensburgh. I had written 'trains', but I didn't notice the error in proof, and the result was that I lost the sales of thousands of copies among Glaswegians. They got really upset about my giving them trams.

"A Mr. Louis Feipal, of Brooklyn, took the trouble to send me a list of 431 errors in one of my novels. They were, in point of fact, nearly all hyphens. I never have been able to follow any particular ruling about hyphens.

"I'm a godsend to the sort of critic who reads a book only with a view to finding misprints. As if my own mistakes were not bad enough, the publishers elected to have a new edition of *Round About England* printed in Holland in 1947.

"A Mr. Millward wrote to the City Librarian, Manchester, the following letter:

"I have just finished reading *Round About England*, by S. P. B. Mais (4 issues) (new book) and enjoyed it. In passing I should like to comment that in all my years of reading I have never met with so many mistakes in spelling and mistype: something like 75 mistakes in 314 pages. I give below the numbers of pages on which the mistakes occur.
Yours truly,
M. A. Millward.

"It's bad enough to get a bad name for inaccuracy when you're at fault, but much worse when you're not at fault."

"It sounds as if you didn't like proof-reading."

"I don't; it's the journeyman's part of the trade of writing, but an author must correct his own proofs.

"They invariably arrive when I'm in the throes of writing another book, and it puts me completely off my stride to have to interrupt my original composition in order to correct proofs which always take an interminable time.

"There's far more to the making of a book than the actual writing, which really costs much less effort than correcting it.

"Incidentally, by far the greatest proportion of my letters are from well-wishers who wish to point out a misprint or an inaccuracy. There are tens of thousands of people whose main occupation is listening for a mis-statement on the air or looking for a misprint in a book. They must derive extraordinary pleasure from my books."

"At any rate it shows you that people do read your books."

"Yes, as Johnson said, it's better to be damned than neglected. I irritate people by my love of fox-hunting and my love of drink. Every time I describe a hunt or the joy I get out of whiskey, mint julep, gin fizz, or a bottle of wine, my post rises to an enormous size. Abuse pours in."

"You don't mind?"

"I've had enough in my time."

"You've said some pretty severe things about public schools. Do you approve of them?"

"Without them the country would go to pieces in no time at all. But until they take the trouble to make boys realize that work for work's sake is the most satisfying thing in the world I shall continue to lash them."

"Not exactly a loyalist, are you?"

"I'm far more loyal than those who find perfection in a system that's very far from perfect. The Church, the Law, and the Schools all need cleaning up, but it appears to be nobody's business to do anything about it."

"Except the Communists."

"Except the Communists, and you do no good by destroying everything. I want reform from within, not destruction from without."

"You think your books have helped to bring about that reform?"

"Well, I've been plain-spoken enough. I've disturbed and shocked people. That's a good thing. I've opened the eyes of others to natural and man-made beauty. That's another thing I'm glad about.

"Through my books I've made many staunch friends and created many enemies. I have been a fervent lover and a good hater. I'm not at all of Landor's opinion. My 'Finis' is exactly the opposite of his. This is mine:

> "I strove with all, for all were worth my strife.
> Nature I fought, and after Nature, Man:
> I burnt both hands before the fire of life:
> It sinks, and I'm among the 'also ran'."

"We can't all be winners. You ran a good race."

"Thank you, Penelope. Unlike Landor, I'm sorry to depart."
The cock crew.

# CHAPTER XV

## I COME BACK TO THE THEATRE (1951)

"YOU'RE early this morning," said Penelope.

I turned in my chair.

"Really, you gave me quite a start," I said. "You see, I've not gone to bed yet."

"It's after two o'clock. That's the time you usually get up."

"I've got a new job."

"It keeps you up late."

"The theatre. It's quite extraordinary the way things are coming full circle in my life. I began by teaching and came back to it after thirty years. I began by writing books and after the B.B.C. finished with me I came back to books."

"In a big way."

"As you say, in a big way. To have over a dozen books coming out this year is a record even for me. I was an undergraduate at Oxford forty-six years ago and here I am a resident again in Oxford. I've been here for ten years and look like dying here. As a journalist I began as a book-reviewer and after twenty years' lapse I again became a journalist, again became a book-reviewer. And now I'm back again in the theatre. I ceased to be a dramatic critic just twenty-five years ago, and here I am once more a dramatic critic. That's why you see me down here at two in the morning on my way to bed, finishing, instead of beginning, my day."

"Does it take all that time to write a notice?"

"I get out of the show at ten o'clock or so, usually have to drive several miles back home. Jill makes me some coffee, then I settle down and some four hours later I've churned out my three hundred words."

"That's slow for you."

"I've got a passion for the theatre. I like to get my notice right. The shorter it is the more difficult it is."

"But that's only once a week, surely."

"No, nearly every night. I only do one professional show—the Repertory Company at the Playhouse—a fortnight on alternate Mondays. The rest of the week I have to go where I'm sent, to amateur shows all over Oxfordshire."

more stupid than the reading public. They're easily shocked. That's why my play *Fog* will never be acted. To come back to these Oxford Repertory Players. I think their choice of play often unfortunate, but they certainly can act They may not make much money, but they do enjoy themselves, and what is more important they communicate their enthusiasm to the audience. There's nothing the matter with my Monday nights. It's the rest of the week that is such a gamble. I'm condemned to travel vast distances at my own expense, and sit on hard seats in draughty ill-equipped halls and watch hard-handed sons of toil struggle on a stage that is too small to throw a cat about in to express emotion in an English that is very far from being the King's. I think it is an excellent thing that farm-hands and shop-assistants should get together and act, because the desire to act is innate in everybody and it helps to form a communal spirit, but they too often choose unsuitable plays. In the last few weeks I have had to sit through grotesque travesties of *The Importance of Being Earnest* and *Hay Fever*. It is silly to expect farmers to interpret Oscar Wilde, and if they must act Noel Coward they should stick to *Fumed Oak*, which they could do perfectly, and not try to ape the manners of the cocktail-drinking lounge-lizards of *Design for Living* and *Hay Fever*. If anything shows the absurdity of pretending that class distinctions and social barriers have been broken down it can be seen by going to any country market-town and watching the efforts of the shopkeepers to hold the mirror up to country-house life."

"But surely the upper classes act too?"

"Undergraduate dramatic societies flourish and I spend half my time watching college plays. These are usually presented with intelligence and the diction is often impeccable, but they too often go wildly astray in their choice of play. I have lately seen Balliol produce an *Uncle Vanya* which the audience elected to treat as another *Charley's Aunt*, and Univ. put on Capek's *Insect Play* which was beyond their power. On the other hand, Trinity gave a good performance of *You Never Can Tell*, and St. Peter's Hall got right inside Aldous Huxley's *The World of Light*."

"What about the girls?"

"They get girl undergraduates, and these finally dispel the fallacy that women undergraduates are thick-ankled, gawky bluestockings. I have lost my heart to at least two in the past two months. They have a tremendous advantage in that they are all young. It is much more satisfying to watch a young undergraduate act the part of an octogenarian than it is to watch a middle-aged woman play the part of Juliet.

"There was a ravishing child in *You Never Can Tell* who answered exactly to Shaw's stage-direction description: 'A very pretty woman in miniature, her tiny figure dressed with the daintiest gaiety—a darling little creature.' "

"What of the girls in the market-towns and villages? Are your emotions roused by them?"

"Not often, for a very obvious reason. The country amateur never forgets the fact that on the morrow he will be back at the bank or collecting tickets at the station or that she will be behind the counter in the haberdashery. Consequently they never really let themselves go emotionally. The love scenes give me a pain in the neck. They find speech bad enough, but they are so conscious of their legs and arms that when they sit down they concentrate solely on not displaying too much leg, and if they are standing up they jerk their arms about as awkwardly as a new recruit handles his rifle. Hands, arms and legs are at least as important a part of an actor's expression as his voice.

"In films, we don't look at the seducer's mouth as he grapples with the reluctant maiden. The kiss may or may not send involuntary shivers of ecstasy down the maiden's spine, but the moment of her surrender is expressed solely through her fingers. First she fights with her fists, then gradually the fists are unclenched and the fingers ever so slowly stretch out towards the villain's coat collar. Suddenly they tighten round his neck and it is she who becomes filled with immortal longings. They can simulate death. They can't simulate love. As most plays are concerned with the journey's end in lovers' meeting, their insipid pecks and half-hearted embraces destroy all sense of illusion. An amateur version of *Romeo and Juliet* would be quite unbearable."

"Don't they ever find a play suitable to their limited talents?"

"I've seen one, at Thame. It was called *The Camel's Back*, by Arnold Helsby. I'd never heard of the play or the author. The problem was one that the actors knew all about. A shrewish middle-aged woman, sister of a recently dead farmer, comes in to take control of her brother's family and farm-hands. She is so beastly that they contrive to find some means of making her go away. Their schemes, all of which are original and funny, all fail until about a minute before the fall of the curtain. The dialogue was brilliant, the acting as good as any professional cast could have produced. They their inability to ring up the curtain at the advertised time. I go without supper in order to be at the place at seven o'clock or whatever time is advertised, and more often than not the curtain doesn't go up till 7.15. A quarter of an hour's a long time when you're sitting on a hard seat in a draught with nothing better to do than listen to the coughs of the audience.

"The intervals are always interminably long. If there was a bar I shouldn't mind, but of course there are no bars in Corn Exchanges or Town Halls. The best I can hope for is coffee. The main refreshment is always ices—ices when it's freezing outside and wind-swept within!"

"You ought to take a thermos."

"I always forget. Better still a flask of brandy. I should like the plays much better if the prompter didn't take the principal part. He's nearly always more audible than any of the cast. Then there is the timing. You'd have thought that even villagers would have picked up a tip or two about timing from the B.B.C. It is invariably too slow, with long awkward pauses during which actors pick up and put down books, the telephone, and glasses of alleged cocktails or whiskey. I remember Aldous Huxley once saying that after a year as a dramatic critic in London he would be ready to enter an asylum. I wonder what he'd make of being a critic of amateur rural dramatic societies."

"You seem to thrive on them."

"I like to encourage people to take an interest in any form of active self-expression. It's better for the soul to act badly than to do football pools well. The theatre, whether it's professional or amateur, is a religion. After all, the play started in the church, and there's a tendency for it to go back to the church. Think of Patric Dickinson's superb *Living Silence* that they broadcast either in or for Liverpool Cathedral, *The Castle of Perseverance* that the Oxford Players acted in St. Mary's Church, *Murder in the Cathedral*, Christopher Fry's *A Sleep of Prisoners* and so on. I'd like to see more amateurs acting morality plays. *Everyman*, for instance. I find myself moved emotionally in almost the same way by a rousing hymn or a good sermon as I am by a good play. The theatre ought to be our great educator. Think what Ibsen and Shaw did to shock us out of conventional morality into common sense, into exercising tolerance and charity. Think how *Hindle Wakes* upset all our ideas about one code of morality for the man and another for the girl. I'm not suggesting that plays should be written with a moral purpose. I do maintain that they should hold the mirror up to life and not be smug or cynical, or outrage our sense of decency and fitness by clapping on an all's-well-that-ends-well finish to an inevitable tragedy like *King Lear* or *Othello*. People don't think. The theatre ought to help us to think."

"You're claiming a lot for the theatre. What about entertainment value?"

"If it hasn't got entertainment value it's nothing, like life without love, an egg without salt. There's room on the stage for pure escapism as well as interpretation. It makes us forget the bankruptcy court, the nagging wife and the ailing child to see a play like *The Man Who Came to Dinner*, *She Stoops to Conquer* or *The Critic*. You get something in the theatre that you never get in the cinema, even in the best Italian pictures. The characters on the stage are as much alive as the characters in a great novel, much more alive than our neighbours, as they reveal so much of themselves, infinitely more alive than the celluloid marionettes on the screen. Think of the comic reality of *The Chiltern Hundreds*, *French Without Tears* and *George and Margaret*, and the sound common sense of *The Linden Tree* and *Laburnum Grove* and *Eden End*. When I was a boy the theatre was looked on as a place of vice. It was taken for granted that all actresses were immoral, all actors promiscuous, and that young men with money hung around the stage doors in order to seduce the chorus girls. It was a charming picture. 'Don't put your daughter on the stage, Mrs. Worthington.' Even today parents are a bit chary about letting their daughters go on the stage.

"I remember as a small boy making friends with a cycle repairer in Matlock Bath. He was the only shopkeeper who didn't speak with a strong Derbyshire accent, so I took it for granted that he was a foreigner. One day he told me that it was his determination to speak English perfectly.

" 'So,' he said, 'I go up to Manchester every early closing day and sit in the gallery of the Gaiety or the Prince of Wales Theatre, not because I care at all about plays. All I do is to listen to every word spoken by the actors and imitate it until I pronounce it as they pronounce it.' It is one of the most striking things about professional actors that they nearly all speak a flawless English untainted by affectation or provincialism. It's a most curious thing that the B.B.C. use voices that are so mannered; think of the critics, think of some announcers, then compare them with Alec Guinness, Ralph Richardson, Eric Portman, Laidman Browne, Carleton Hobbs and Gladys Young. Generally speaking it is a delight to hear

# CHAPTER XVI

## I Go Back To Europe (1947–51)

"I think you're the most unpredictable person I've ever known," said Penelope.

"What way am I unpredictable? You always find me at my desk at three in the morning."

"It's not that. Do you remember at Cranwell refusing to let someone fly you back home because you were afraid of the air?"

"I do."

"And yet when it came to flying over Cromarty Firth to Orkney in an aeroplane that was just a piece of sticking-paper and string and a pilot that only knew the Andes you were as excited as a small child?"

"I do."

"And do you remember that you once dreaded the sea so much that you daren't face the steamer trip from Ilfracombe to Lundy?"

"I do."

"And yet you gaily set off last Winter to cross the Bay of Biscay and were the only person not sick, and last Summer across the North Sea and up through the Arctic Circle as far as the North Cape, and again were the only person not sick?"

"Not as far as the North Cape. Only Tromsö. Well, what of it?"

"Just unpredictability, that's all. What was the reason for this sudden decision to invade Europe and go dashing off to Madeira and Norway?"

"To make money. The B.B.C. had given me my *congé*. I had finished schoolmastering. I had no means of livelihood. I had exhausted England, Scotland, Wales and Ireland. I had already returned to all these and made a considerable profit out of my books, notably on Scotland, and my publisher was willing to advance £200 to pay my expenses getting material out of tourist countries abroad. So I went. The countries themselves were glad to have me and provided transport facilities and either reduced terms or free hospitality in their hotels, not only for me but also for Jill, Lalage and Imogen."

"What a racket! I don't wonder you cashed in on that. A holiday

172

with pay. That's very neat. I didn't know that you were such a good business man."

"When you owe the bank £2,500 you've got to become a good business man or go broke. I've not been doing it long. Only four years. It was in 1947 that we went to Montreux. There was an added inducement to go abroad then. I determined not to repeat the mistake that I had made when I wasted £100 in taking the family to Ilfracombe. I wanted sun, good food, good drink, water warm enough to bathe in, blue skies, a change from the ghastly sort of visitor that was now overrunning all the English seaside resorts. So we went to Montreux. I had been to Switzerland before, but not for twenty-four years, and then in the Winter for the ski-ing.

"I have never made a wiser decision. Switzerland is the best holiday-ground in the world at any time of the year.

"Quite apart from anything else it was essential for me to get right away from Oxford for at least one month in every three, for the climate was rapidly destroying not only my health but that of Jill and the children. It must be easily the worst climate in the world, and the Winter of 1947 is not one that anyone will easily forget. We had had sixteen weeks of unprecedented hard frosts, gales, floods and a sky that was always grey.

"The sight of the snow-covered Alps and the Mediterranean blue of the Lake of Geneva acted like an electric shock. I was a different person within an hour. The cleanliness, the prosperity, the smiling faces, the lovely food, the cheap and good Rhône Valley wines, all combined to put me, as Pepys would say, in a very good conceit of myself.

"We set off to explore the Saanen Valley and I had my first experience of a ski-hoist, which frightened me nearly out of my wits. It was the one from Gstaad to the Wasserngrat which climbs 2,000 feet in about twenty interminable minutes. I shut my eyes and sweated with fear the whole way up. But at the top, at a height of 5,500 feet, we had luncheon out of doors in our shirt-sleeves. 'I want to stay here for ever,' said Imogen, voicing what we all felt. I shall never forget that view. We were right in the heart of the Alps and could see in the distance the great bluff of Mont Blanc, the Mönch, Eiger and Jungfrau, the Diablerets and the Wildhorn. Talk about ecstasy! I felt as the disciples felt on the Mount of Transfiguration. We were transfigured all right.

"It was roses, roses all the way. It was better than that. We lay in beds of amaranthine flowers; the fields were a sea of crocuses and

"We first visited the Castle of Monaco and the wonderful aquarium and admired the wealth of bougainvillaeas everywhere. Oranges and lemons grow in the streets of Menton. The next day we explored Nice, which is much too large for my liking. The shops are good and there are several ritzy hotels, but as a place I much prefer Brighton, to which it bears some resemblance.

"We drove up into the mountains behind Nice to have luncheon at Valberg, which is a winter-sports centre, but can't hold a candle to the Swiss winter resorts. Every hotel is just a glorified chalet and there are practically no shops at all.

"One day we crossed the border into Italy to visit San Remo, where we were grossly overcharged for a none too good luncheon and a bottle of chianti. It was terrifically hot and we were too tired to explore the town. There is far more to see in Menton, which has an ancient quarter with narrow cobbled streets and tall dark tenement houses with green shutters and washing hanging across the road. The wonderful cathedral is in this mediaeval section of the town.

"We drove to Tende, a remote village high up in the hills, which was first French, then taken by the Germans, handed over to Italy, and is now French again.

"The mountain roads are magnificent. They run through a succession of tunnels blasted through the rock above stupendous narrow gorges.

"Jill was turned out of the cathedral by two nuns because she was wearing shorts. This caused her to burst into tears. Half an hour later she was turned out of another church by a priest and a monk. That made me so angry that I became very voluble (in English) while the priest and the monk stood silent and still in the middle of the aisle.

"On this journey we passed many German cemeteries. The fighting in the mountain passes round Tende had been severe. We could see bullet marks on the cowsheds and rusty German helmets hanging above the haycocks. We stopped for a time at Sospel on this excursion. Its main characteristic is its foul smell. It had been badly smashed by the Germans.

"We sailed to the islands of St. Marguerite, where the Man in the Iron Mask was imprisoned, and St. Honoret, where I was taken over the Cistercian Abbey where no women are allowed, while Jill and Imogen explored the eleventh-century fortress castle. There were cicadas in both islands, making a tremendous noise. On the way back we stopped at Cannes long enough for us to take in the fact that it was smart and expensive. You have to pay exorbitant sums to lie on or bathe from any of the many little lidos or beaches.

"All the girls were bronzed and practically naked. I saw Cartier's shop window, which contained one colossal diamond tiara, and Worth's, which contained just one floppy hat. Cannes reeks of money. It is not garish, but it is exhibitionist. The harbour was crowded with millionaires' private steam yachts. The Carlton is certainly the most expensive-looking hotel I ever set eyes on. I felt no desire to stay in Cannes.

"I much preferred the look of Juan-les-Pins and Cap d'Antibes. We passed the villas belonging to the Duke of Windsor, Rita Hayworth, Maurice Chevalier, Mistinguett and a number of other celebrities. Life at Cap d'Antibes must be vastly different from life at Menton. I was glad that we were staying at Menton.

"We had been advised to stay at La Napoule, a little to the west of Cannes, so we went to inspect it and found that it contained two expensive small hotels, each with its private beach. Two restaurants refused to let us eat our packed lunches on their premises, so we found a restaurant just behind the station where the proprietor was more forthcoming. There is a public beach but it was full of ants, dirty sand and litter, and overcrowded, so we decided that La Napoule was napoo for us and went back to Cannes, where Imogen and I undressed on a free beach and swam into the millionaires' water, which tasted just the same. The bathing millionaires in their short bathing trunks looked, as Nancy Mitford would say, just like the cups growing out of acorns, fat and repulsive. Most of them were speaking in a broad Scots brogue and they were definitely not swimming. They were standing thigh deep. Imogen and I waded ashore and strolled up and down the private Carlton beach and had a good laugh at the millionaires and their odd lady friends.

" 'It's just like an American musical,' said Imogen. She noticed that the water was dirtier than it is at Menton. In Jill's view Cannes is tawdry, vulgar and trashy. That, I think, is an accurate summary.

"I much preferred Monte Carlo, where we spent the next day, though the Casino was the only place in the whole of the Côte d'Azur where I saw people with careworn faces. There was an extraordinary old woman at one of the tables. She was a hunchback with white hair, her cheeks were rose-tinted and she wore a floppy lilac straw hat and stood up all the time taking notes of all the numbers that came up at the roulette table. She put no chips on.

"I think nothing of the Casino, but the town of Monte Carlo is

M

"There was an exquisite Greek girl and a fair-haired Norwegian bride who were very easy on the eye.

"But it was the cold table at luncheon that I remember best. It consisted of pork, ham, caviare, smoked salmon, *pâté de foie gras*, cold chicken, Russian salad, olives, sardines, anchovies, shrimps, eggs, brawn, liver pie, mixed grill and mimosa.

"That was only the *hors-d'œuvre*. It was followed by a six-course meal. I drank a large number of gins and Italian, and whiskies and ginger ale. There was a shop on board where Jill, Imogen and Lalage spent much time when they were feeling up to it. I bought these Norwegian sealskin slippers there.

"I love the sea. I love striding on the top deck in the early morning when there's nobody else about except the ship's boys swabbing. It was wonderful to be going south with the temperature rising all the time. I didn't care how rough it was. We were chased by a hurricane all the way.

"It took five days to reach Funchal, which is one of the most lovely places in the world. It consists of thousands of white houses dotted about among trees on a steep mountain-side.

"We arrived about midnight, when it was all lit up, and the ship was surrounded by small boats from which small naked boys dived into the clear water for the coins we threw down. We went ashore at breakfast-time and I was first of all struck by the bougainvillaea, strelitsia, golden-rod and cactus, and the lizards flashing about all the crannies in the walls. It felt tropical all right. I fell in love with Madeira the moment I set foot on it. I liked the ox wagons with their attendants all dressed in white and straw hats bound with Cambridge-blue ribbons. I liked the pretty, slender-legged, black-haired, brown-eyed girls who smiled so amiably.

"I liked the shops, full of silk nighties, silverwork, wood-work, embroidery, and of course Madeira wine.

"There were buses going all over the island, but we found Funchal much too exciting to tear ourselves away from the shops except to bathe. It was wonderful to be able to bathe in the sea on Christmas Day. The water was not quite so warm as the Mediter-ranean but it was warm enough. There were two swimming-pools, one at Reid's, one at the Savoy, and we used them indiscriminately.

"We went over an embroidery factory and a wine stores and drank quantities of different brands of Madeira. We were enter-tained in country houses of great magnificence.

"The natives are primitive and poor and superstitious but quite happy. They smile easily. They walk about barefooted and carry immense loads on their shoulders.

"We attended the Christmas Midnight High Mass in the cathedral, which was packed to overflowing, but the highspot was the firework display with which they celebrate the arrival of the New Year. The whole sky was ablaze with magnificent rockets. I have never seen such a display. For the rest we bathed and danced and drank and ate prodigiously, and were taken for a couple of drives up into the mountains.

"The children came down one of the mountains on toboggans. I was ill that day. The weather wasn't kind. It rained. We had a hurricane, but I loved it all in spite of the weather.

"We went on to Teneriffe on New Year's Day. I thought nothing of Santa Cruz or the Spanish. The dogs were dying of hunger. The men spat. The girls scowled. The place stank. There was one magnificent church, the Church of the Immaculate Conception, with ornate silverwork and a flag captured from Nelson. I was glad to get back to the cleanliness of the *Venus*.

"The voyage home was uneventful. I won the sweep on the day's run of the ship and lost on 'Housy-housy' and drank a lot and ate a lot and felt fighting fit. The others were sick. I never missed a single meal going out or coming back!

"We spent the Summer holidays of 1950 doing a trip of seven or eight thousand miles up to Tromsö, down to Oslo and back to Bergen. It was my first visit to Norway. I propose never to go back. Give me the south and the sun.

"Norway isn't tourist-minded. There's nothing to drink. It's expensive. The people seldom smile. The mountains and fjords are terrific, and that's all there is to be said about it.

"This time I was given £250 in advance by Donald Johnson, and the Bergen Steamship Co. gave me a free passage and free hotel accommodation. And yet it cost about £200.

"We went out in the *Venus* (the same ship in which we had sailed to Madeira but now altered to accommodate about 700 passengers instead of 250). We sailed from Newcastle on the Saturday before Bank Holiday and the ship was uncomfortably full.

"The voyage across the North Sea takes twenty-three hours. It was dull going out and very stormy coming back, yet once more I didn't miss a meal either way, though Jill and Imogen (we left Lalage behind) were both violently ill.

"I got my first unpleasant surprise at Bergen. It was infinitely and when we reached Videseter for luncheon she fell into my arms on getting out of the bus. I was sweating with fright. We drove on through a less frightful country to Lom Fellstue, which is a new wooden hotel beautifully situated about 4,000 feet up on a plateau overlooking two valleys. That drive was about 200 miles. The next day we did a climb on our own. It was the last day we were to enjoy the sun.

"A car was sent to take us over a wild waste of craters, snow-fields and fjords below a gigantic glacier to Grinde (another 200 miles), where we caught a ferry which took us to the Kvikne Hotel, Balestrand, the largest hotel in Western Norway and packed with English and American visitors. It was a barracks-like building right above the jetty. It was there that I first saw anyone in Norway drinking sherry.

"We spent a couple of days walking along the shores of the fjord. The mountains here were less intimidating than at Geiranger, but it rained a lot and we couldn't do much. We were reduced to attending Evensong at the English church.

"We went on by steamer to Flaam, a four-hour voyage. Some passengers changed steamer in mid-fjord, which was exciting. We got to Fretheim about ten o'clock at night and found a pleasant hotel which had once been a country house. The next morning we climbed by electric train up a precipitous line overlooking a deep gorge to Myrdal, where we joined the Bergen-Oslo express, in which we spent eight hours looking out through blinding rain into wild snowfields. We stopped at Finse, the highest railway station in Europe, to see the place where Scott and his men came to train for that last fatal Antarctic Expedition. I felt that if they could endure Finse they could endure anything. I was glad when we at last began the long descent to the gentler timber country.

"We got to Oslo late that night and it was still raining.

"Oslo is quite a place. The hotel was the most expensive I have ever stayed in, but the food was good and we could get wine.

"We were taken to see the Folk Museum, where there are replicas of all the old farms, which impressed me more than ever with the primitiveness of the country. We saw Nansen's ship, the *Fram*, and within a hundred yards of it the raft *Kon-Tiki*. We also saw five Viking ships and the amazing Vigeland statues in the Vigeland Park. That was the highspot of our tour. I was by this time almost passing out. We had to take the train back some 300 miles to Geilo, which is a winter sports resort. The only saving grace was a wonderful mountain walk behind the hotel. Forests covered the whole valley. We were driven on from Geilo by the nicest man we met in Norway, Mr. Wehn, the manager of the bus company, who came over in an enormous American car and drove us over wild wastes with glaciers all round and nothing else except snowfields, boulders and fjords. We stopped for luncheon at Fossli, where we looked over a precipice at a waterfall that is more impressive than Niagara. We had to descend a fearful gorge and I was thankful to reach the level of the sea fjords. He took us across the fjord from Kvandal to Norheimsund. By that time we had covered over 300 miles and there was no room for us at the inn. So he drove us a further ten miles up into the mountains to a Sater hut.

"The next day we went back to Norheimsund. By that time I had had a surfeit of mountains and fjords. The three of us drooled miserably round the edge of the water and longed for home.

"We had to waste two whole days there before going on by bus for the last mountain drive to Bergen. In Bergen we wasted two more days. We saw Grieg's home and were taken to Solstrand for a superb luncheon in the worst storm within living memory.

"The next day we set sail for home in a hurricane. Jill and Imogen were more sick than I have ever seen anybody at sea or on land.

"We made up for that mistake at Christmas. We returned to Switzerland and again I got a publisher to advance £200 and prevailed upon the Swiss authorities to provide free facilities over their railways and free hotel accommodation for ten days at Wengen and ten days at Gstaad. We had the worst journey out that I have ever had. I told you about that journey.

"It couldn't have been a more unpropitious start. To add to it I had been ill ever since I came back from Norway. Yet within twenty-four hours I was on top of the world and stayed there.

"The sun came out. We could see the Mönch, the Eiger and the Jungfrau from our bedroom window, as well as the deep gorge of Lauterbrunnen.

"Imogen and I hired skis and from that moment we were in heaven. We went out on to the nursery slopes. I stayed on the nursery slopes. Imogen was luckier. I discovered that my friend Douglas McNair's wife and son Philip were staying at the Regina and Philip took Imogen up to the Bumps and brought her down. That gave her the jolt of her life because it was all icefield. There had been scarcely any snow.

# CHAPTER XVII

## L'ENVOI: THANKS FOR THE MEMORY (1937–51)

(1) THE sight and smell of wild thyme bring back a fragrant and lovely memory.

When Jill and I first met we spent halcyon days walking over the South Downs in the sun. We didn't walk all the time. We lay down on the close-cropped grass looking out over the sunlit sea. In June we uprooted bits of wild thyme and gave them to each other. I have mine still. She was seventeen and I was thirty-seven.

(2) Whenever I smell *eau-de-Cologne*, or for that matter camphor, I am transported to my childhood and my mother. She drenched herself and her notepaper with the former and applied the latter to her chest and nose with the assiduity of a drug addict. I must have loved my mother inordinately because those two scents give me a warm, comfortable, cosy feeling, as cosy, comfortable and warm as the feeling induced by the peculiar and very faint smell that I get in all large and old country houses. I suppose it is partly the smell of old oak. Whatever it is, it reminds me of the two Devon farms, Yarde and Boode, where I spent much of my lonely childhood under the aegis of two maiden aunts who neither spared the rod nor spoilt the child.

(3) My family and I have a standing annual bet of five shillings as to who shall hear the first cuckoo, see the first swallow, and pick the first cowslip. Usually all three occur on the same day, between the 7th and 14th April.

But the cuckoo, swallow and cowslip always take me back to those far distant Easters when Jill was in her teens and I nearing forty. Always we went to Chagford, ate lashings of Devonshire cream, walked up the Wallabrook to Cranmere, and down the Teign to Fingle Bridge.

(4) There were curlew on Dartmoor and there is no sound more haunting than the call of the curlew over the moor at Easter, but it is not of Chagford that I think when I hear that exquisite melody but of Llanwrtyd.

(5) The smell of mud and wet leaves encountered when we are following hounds on foot takes me back to undergraduate days when I ran across country and thought that the gaining of a Blue was of all earthly things the thing I coveted most.

Mud-wet leaves are to me a symbol of terrific endeavour.

(6) To me it is a source of great exhilaration to hear the howling of the wind round the house, and takes me back to days of early childhood, when I used to look out of my bedroom window at Boode during the great westerly gales and watch the waves piling high in Barnstaple Bay and the lights of Lundy glittering away far out at sea. Walking in a high wind, especially on the tops of mountains, puts me into a good mood with myself and the rest of the world.

(7) Of all the sounds that I dread, that of the sirens comes easily first. It reminds me of Lalage and Imogen coming under machine-gun fire every day at Shoreham on their way home to luncheon, tea and supper.

Between the sound of the sirens and the dropping of the first bomb is a dreadful interim when our ears are all keyed up and nerves jangled.

Whenever I hear a siren I think of those strange walks at two o'clock in the morning when, after broadcasting to America, I had to make my way from 200 Oxford Street to the Cumberland. The street was of course deserted, the only noise would be that of leaves being swept along by the wind and telephones ringing in the empty air, the only visible sight that of scores of twinkling green traffic lights and a stray cat or two noiselessly making its way across the road.

Sirens sounded nightly wherever we went, in our home at Shoreham, in my father's rectory in Derbyshire, especially on the night of the Coventry raid, and in our hotel at Bristol where I was broadcasting. There was no escape from the sirens, no escape from the ensuing bombs. It is a dreary wail and appropriate to its function.

(8) I doubt very much whether there is a lovelier smell on earth than that of the stable when horses are being harnessed. I have ridden all my life and that smell takes me back to the farm at Yarde when my uncle used to drive me from one farm to another, to the riding stables at Woolacombe where Jill, Lalage and Imogen used to ride, and to the stables in Oxford where I now ride.

(9) The music of the anvil draws me invariably to enter every smithy that I pass on my walks, when I stand and gape as horses are fitted for their shoes with infinitely more care than any shoemaker ever bestowed upon mine.

All craftsmen are worth watching. The contrast between those who work for money, toiling and moiling with their eye on the tall elms gradually creeping up to the pitch, I see cows grazing in the buttercup-tinged long grass and in their midst the long field. I see trestle-tables under the trees with white tablecloths and a shining urn (no tea in the world is so welcome and so satisfying as tea in the interval). I see the village ancients bowed low sitting on the benches that surround the field, I see youngsters chasing each other between these benches. I see a white mast and myself standing with my pads on trying strokes that I shall never employ when I get out there.

Alas, for me it is all over. I have played for the last time, bowled ignominiously by a mite of a boy in the Fathers' match at the Dragon before I had scored. I was over-eager (the bowler's name was Eager) to shine before two of the spectators (Lalage and Imogen).

> The field is full of shades as I near the shadowy coast,
> And a ghostly batsman plays to the bowling of a ghost,
> And I look through my tears on a soundless-clapping host
> As the run-stealers flicker to and fro,
>                 To and fro:
> O my Hornby and my Barlow long ago.

If I am privileged as a ghost to revisit the glimpses of the moon perhaps you'd like my address. It will be:

The Village Green,
Southwick,
Sussex.

And I'll tell you where exactly on the green I shall be in case you want to exchange greetings. I shall be hovering over the oak seat which bears the inscription:

"Given by Lalage and Imogen Mais."

That is, if the Government haven't requisitioned it for fuel.
I shall be there even if the seat has been stolen.
I'll be seeing you, but you won't be seeing me.
So "Good-bye for now."

# APPENDIX A

## I Was a Poet Once

### Dawn on Dartmoor

Away to th' East beyond Yes Tor a light
Like apple, green to russet, doth unfold,
And Earth discards the beauteous web of Night
Trembling with ecstasy at this birth of gold,
Her garment fresh, now myriad-rayed inspires
The cock to crow and joyous birds to sing.
All living creatures now take up their lyres
To praise their God, Good Luck on Man to bring:
But sweeter still the "burr" of accent soft
When happy milkmaid, rosy-faced, trips out
To wake the sleeper in the neighbour croft
With "Marnin', zur, 'tis taime yew'm waake about."
Pure virgin souls, here's proof man cannot miss:
Thy county and thyself alone received God's kiss.

### Dusk in Derbyshire

O! country of grey walls and greyer skies,
How ill dost thou affect thy native youth:
No sounds of laughter to the welkin rise;
No merry, careless cheer; but all uncouth
Neighbour greets neighbour with a gruff salute,
And on the stranger casts a hostile glare:
To eager questioning remains all mute
Like beast at graze or tired-out, hunted hare.
Yet Beauty, if we search for her, is here;
Crags towering o'er the river far below,
Trees sparse and wan on mountain-tops appear
Pointing out tombs of giants on the Low.
But desolate is the region for the soul,
For no birds sing, and all men seek Death's goal.

### Education

And who's to blame for this? So young, so fair,
So innocent-seeming, yet so false to God,

N

His own ideals, his people and—is't rare?—
His bosom friend; it can't be true he trod
The paths of vice full knowing; who's to blame?
I, you and everyone. Shall we then expel,
Wash our hands, guiltless—we, who choose to maim
For life, perhaps beyond, a boy who fell
Because we couldn't reach him, didn't try,
Or some such damn'd excuse, the last one right.
Expel him? Yes, by all means. Guilty? Why
Of course: it's proved: and by the guiding light
Of our school rules he must for others' sake
Depart at once. Quite so—a piece of cake?

### The Ponies

The foals they were a-playing,
Upon a sunny day,
Their mothers stood a-neighing
In case they stole away.

But when the night began to fall
The foals lay down to sleep,
Their mothers stood around them all
And by them, safely keep.

*By* LALAGE.

# APPENDIX B

## FAREWELL TO TEACHING

IN September 1940, after exactly twenty years' absence, I went back to the classroom. In November, after exactly half a term, I went out again, for, I imagine, the last time. I was not, surprisingly, sacked. I left, for once, of my own volition.

The reasons? Partly because I was mistaken in my belief that I was really wanted to relieve a younger man for military service. The younger schoolmasters are, quite rightly, staying where they are. But my main reason for leaving was that I seemed to be wasting my own time and that of the boys.

I suffered an extremely rude awakening. For twenty years I have lived in a fool's paradise. I believed that I was once a good schoolmaster, that I had a vocation for teaching and that all the windmills against which I had tilted before the last war had been swept away. As a result I longed to go back now that all the reforms that I had advocated and suffered for in the long ago had been achieved. What fun, I thought, to teach boys who really wanted to know, without the spur of reward or the fear of punishment! What fun, I thought, no longer to have to try to standardize every pupil into a successful candidate for the School or Higher Certificate, but to encourage each boy to develop his own latent talents in his own way!

You see, I had read a lot about the trend of modern education. My only fear was lest I should not be able to keep abreast of the modern ways of arousing enthusiasm and be ridiculed for falling back on obsolete methods.

I need not have worried. It was the school, it was the classroom, that was obsolete. I had to rub my eyes to make sure that I was not Rip Van Winkle as I entered that classroom for the first time. Everything was the same as it had been in 1920, and everything was wrong. The room was bare and ugly with not a picture or a flower anywhere, the desks the acme of discomfort, the blackboard as pitted with holes as any No-Man's-Land, the chalk evasive, the cleaner a nightmare, the text-books stereotyped and unimaginative, the boys listless, careless and ignorant beyond belief.

I found myself in charge of the English of a form whose sole reason for existence was that every one of the boys had failed in the School Certificate and was due to take it again at the end of the term. Their attitude to their "special book", *Twelfth Night*, coincided with that of Pepys ("the play doth seem a burthen to me, and I took no pleasure at all in it"), and they were more than shocked when I suggested that if they took no pleasure in their set books there must be something radically wrong with the way they read them.

There was. They took a year reading one play and two other books, and they spent the greater part of that time learning up the introduction and the notes and "likely" passages for paraphrase.

When I suggested that the only way to pass examinations was not to treat them too seriously, and that the only way to tackle a play was to act it as if you meant to put it over to an audience as an entertainment, I was regarded by half the form as a dangerous revolutionary and by the other half as falling into senile decay.

I paid the Sixth Form the compliment (which they were incapable of appreciating) of treating them as undergraduates in order to encourage free discussion and wide reading on subjects of more vital interest to the citizen than the don, and found that their ignorance of civics and aesthetics was as profound as their distaste for them. They lolled back in their seats and went to sleep.

They had read nothing and had no desire to read anything. As the school library was almost barren that was not entirely their fault. Indeed, it is easier to find the root of the fault in the parents than in the system for the extraordinary travesty that was passing under the name of education.

First, the parents. Alphabeta is not in the first flight of Public Schools. It could make no claim to tradition as Winchester does. It attracted the farmers and shopkeepers who wished to assert a little social superiority over their neighbours who were content with the free and secondary schools. They didn't care, presumably, whether the actual education was better or worse. Presumably as they were paying more they took it for granted that it would be better. But what they were paying for in reality was a veneer. These minor so-called Public Schools trade on and exist by the Englishman's innate snobbery.

I lay the blame primarily on the parents for not caring enough about education as such. They didn't want their boys to be interested in citizenship or art. In other words, they weren't interested in their sons' ability either to use their leisure profitably or even to aim at a different profession or trade. There would always be the shop or the farm for the boy to fall back on. As for his leisure, there would always be football to watch or football pools when he was past playing the game. So they never even want to claim their money back when they find that at eighteen their sons can't even spell, punctuate or string two sentences together logically.

I could scarcely believe my eyes when I first looked at my time-sheet and at the faces in my form. Neither the hours nor the numbers had altered in any particular since the last war. I was expected to teach classes of twenty-six to twenty-eight boys for twenty-six to twenty-eight hours every week. If I had ten boys to teach for ten hours a week I might have achieved something in spite of the parents.

But alas, with age I have cultivated a conscience. In the old days when I was a master at Tonbridge I told my boys that I would select one per cent of their preparation haphazard for correction. To show my contempt for the punishment system I made one boy learn the whole of *The Ancient Mariner* (it took him a term) for leaving the door open once, and refused to punish a boy at all who absented himself from class for a whole week on the ground that he could get on better by himself. He was quite right. To show my contempt for the mark system I would give 1½ million marks for a monosyllabic "Yes" (and a guess at that) and 0·25 of a mark for a long essay. At Sherborne I frequently told my form to teach themselves while I went on writing at my desk. They never learnt more.

But in old age I found myself conforming to impossible rules. I really tried for seven weeks to correct and comment upon all the written work done by my various forms and sets. It left me no time at all to prepare original lessons or to set original preparation.

I have always maintained that each form in conjunction with its form master should write its own text-books day by day as it goes along. I immediately discovered the impossibility of doing that. In my Mathematical Set I was assigned particular sections of particular text-books to cover in the term. The ground was absurdly small. Most of the boys had done it all before, were completely disillusioned about the whole thing, and only wanted to be let alone to work out a thousand variations of the stereotyped problem solved for them at the top of the page.

When I attempted to turn my mathematical classes into discussions and essays in English, and turned my English classes into discussions and essays on mathematical abstractions, there was the devil to pay. It was bad enough to have a master who refused to keep Algebra, Arithmetic and Geometry in separate watertight compartments, but when it came to using opposite, adjacent, corresponding and alternate angles as an introduction to all possible uses of the words opposite, adjacent, corresponding and alternate the thing was going just a bit too far. They became stolid, passive resisters *en bloc*.

Now if I fail to arouse interest I'm done. I cannot turn myself into a wet nurse and slap a boy when he sneezes. An appalling thing happened. I lost interest too.

I just couldn't do with boys who failed to find anything exciting in St. Exupéry flying, Cherry Garrard's *Worst Journey*, or Housman's lyrics. I have every sympathy with a boy's resistance to stereotyped education. I have no sympathy whatever with a boy who refuses to take any interest in the world about him.

I remembered Lancelot Hogben's startling indictment: "The two indispensable talents (for teachers) are: for a woman, chastity, and for a man, football." As a young man I had spent years of invaluable time chasing footballs and exhorting boys to chase footballs. Now I couldn't even bear to stand on the touchline and watch these boys because of the contrast. They played football well. It was the only thing they could do, and the staff all applauded and yelled wildly as they stamped their cold feet on the sodden earth.

Perhaps in girls' schools there is the same unrestrained enthusiasm for virginity, though I doubt whether it is such an obsession as football is in boys' schools. For girls find time to be enthusiastic about poetry as well as chastity, and I have never found so receptive or so responsive an audience as the average girls' school.

So it may be a solution to introduce masters into girls' schools, though I have an idea that girls have a natural curiosity about things intellectual and aesthetic, anyway, and I also have an idea that education in girls' schools has improved considerably in its breadth of outlook since the last war, whereas education in boys' schools has slipped back.

Whatever the reason, I found myself incapable of making those easy and delightful friendships with boys that made my earlier years of schoolmastering so happy. I found the conversation of these boys tedious to a degree. I could not even bear to ask them out to tea.

I was myself cut off from the whole outer world of man with no time left to read, to keep abreast of news, and no time left to write, to air my own views. I was just a prisoner penned in a singularly uncomfortable cell with uncongenial company. I was underpaid (£300 a year) and overworked. I had made the startling discovery that youth is best served by youth.

It was bad enough to be bored by the boys, but I was equally out of touch with my colleagues, nearly all of whom were young enough to be my sons. Most of them seemed to me to be serving their time on a treadmill, and degenerating into slaves of a system for which I can find no defence.

If the war didn't shake this type of minor Public School into drastic changes it will probably (I hope) shake it out of existence. Not even the most enlightened and ardent headmaster can do anything against a Board of Governors looking for economic stability before educational reform, and I feel desperately sorry for keen educationalists caught in this trap.

(Reprinted from the *New Statesman*, by kind permission of the Editor.)

## APPENDIX C

### I Stand Corrected

26 Ernocroft Road,
Ludworth,
Marple Bridge.
5th January.

Dear Sir,

```
I   I   I   I   I   I   I   I   I   I   I   I
I   I   I   I   I   I   I   I   I   I   I   I
I   I   I   I   I   I   I   I   I   I   I   I
I   I   I   I   I   I   I   I   I   I   I   I
I   I   I   I   I   I   I   I   I   I   I   I
I   I
```

me    me    me    me    me    me    me    me    me
me    me    me    me    me    me    me
my    my    my    my    my    my    my    my    my
my    my    my    my    my    my    my    my    my
my    my    my    my    my    my    my

Very shyly I am sending you the above supply of personal pronouns for use in your next article for the *Radio Times*. They *all* appeared in your last one. If you doubt it, here is an analysis:

| Sentences containing | 0 | personal pronouns (I, me or my) | 16 |
|---|---|---|---|
| ,, | ,, | 1 ,,        ,,        ,, | 23 |
| ,, | ,, | 2 ,,        ,,        ,, | 21 |
| ,, | ,, | 3 ,,        ,,        ,, | 3 |
| ,, | ,, | 4 ,,        ,,        ,, | 1 |
| ,, | ,, | 5 ,,        ,,        ,, | 2 |
| ,, | ,, | 6 ,,        ,,        ,, | 1 |
| ,, | ,, | 9 ,,        ,,        ,, | 1 |

Total sentences: 68. Total personal pronouns used: 103.

Sentences without reference to S. P. B. Mais: 16.

Sentences referring to S. P. B. Mais: 52.

Please do not imagine that I have any antipathy to the personal pronouns. Some of the best writers use quite as many as you. But they usually manage to hang something memorable to them. Personal pronouns in their hands are the gateway to impersonal truth or beauty. One ends up by forgetting the pronoun and seeing the beauty.

Where exactly were your personal pronouns meant to lead one in last week's *Radio Times*? I would really like to know because in a world so full of distraction as ours every writer who merely fills space to distract men's attention for the *sake* of distracting is cheapening the art he claims to serve.

And when such a distractor has a voice or a sympathetic touch which, on his own admission, gets the best applause from girls' schools, he ought to be careful how he is using them. Better a millstone . . . than that young people at an impressionable age should learn to love that personal pronoun for its own sake.

Yours sincerely,

J. E. BEAN.

# APPENDIX D

## DID EVER MAN HAVE TRUER FRIENDS?

*Marks awarded to those friends who answered my questionnaire in "Do You Know?"*

*Maximum* 100

| | |
|---|---|
| 1. H. H. Hardy | 98 |
| 2. Compton Mackenzie | 92 |
| 3. Sir Arthur Quiller Couch | 90 |
| 4. Beachcomber ⎫ | |
|     Nowell Smith ⎬ | 82 |
|     Will Owen ⎭ | |
| 7. Lady Eleanor Smith | 80 |
| 8. Ian Hay | 76 |
| 9. W. B. Maxwell | 75 |
| 10. Henry Ainley ⎫ | |
|     Sir William Beech Thomas ⎬ | 74 |
|     Sir Jack Squire ⎭ | |
| 13. James Agate ⎫ | |
|     St. John Ervine ⎭ | 72 |
| 15. Sir Theodore Cook | 71 |
| 16. Olga Lindo | 70 |
| 17. Gilbert Frankau | 69 |
| 18. Aldous Huxley | 68 |
| 19. Margaret Kennedy | 65 |
| 20. Owen Nares | 64 |
| 21. Storm Jameson | 64 |

| | |
|---|---|
| 22. H. G. Wells | 63 |
| 23. J. F. Roxburgh ⎫ | |
|     R. D. Blumenfeld ⎬ | 62 |
|     John Galsworthy ⎭ | |
| 26. Athene Seyler ⎫ | |
|     Sybil Thorndike ⎬ | 60 |
|     Sir Ian Hamilton ⎭ | |
| 29. Sir Osbert Sitwell | 59 |
| 30. Nicholas Hannen | 56 |
| 31. Harold Abrahams | 55 |
| 32. C. R. W. Nevinson ⎫ | |
|     George Grossmith ⎬ | 54 |
| 34. Sir Harry Preston | 53 |
| 35. Judge Parry | 49 |
| 36. Alec Waugh* | 45 |
| 37. Lena Ashwell | 44 |
| 38. Arthur Young* | 41 |
| 39. Noel Coward | 39 |
| 40. Beverley Nichols ⎫ | |
|     P. C. Wren ⎬ | 34 |
| 42. Mrs. Belloc Lowndes | 33 |

*\* Ex-pupils of mine!*

# APPENDIX E

## TAILPIECE

### *S for Sugar*

INTERVIEWER, 1951: Tell me, Mr. Mais, have you ever thought of writing a book?

S. P. B. M.: Yes.